About the Author

Jack Collis grew up in the small New South Wales country town of Ganmain. He ran his own business for 16 years until he joined AMP as a salesman, receiving the AMP's award for the best new salesman recruited in NSW that year. After three years he moved into AMP management, and 14 years later, after acting as Sales Manager of AMP-Queensland and then Sales Manager of AMP-New South Wales, he was moved to Head Office as Marketing Manager for the Society. He held this position for three years until he left AMP to pursue his other business interests.

Jack is now a full-time international speaker and author. He owns and runs a very successful speaking and consulting business and produces a range of books, training and development programs for business, including his recently developed Business Master Class executive coaching program.

His book *Work Smarter Not Harder*, co-authored with Michael LeBoeuf, has been translated into three languages. *Yes You Can*, his mind, time and goals book, has been published in two languages, and his *The Great Sales Book* has become the authority on selling in Australia and was recently published in South-East Asia and India.

Jack is a recognised leader in the fields of personal development, mindpower and creative marketing.

The International Management Centres Association of Revans University in Great Britain recently conferred on Jack an honorary Doctor of Management degree for his worldwide contribution to management.

What Others Say About Jack's Presentations

Jack Collis is an inspiration . . . what he says hits home with such power. We need people like Jack to kick us out of our mental ruts, to lift our sights and put us on track for the breakthroughs we are looking for.

Michael Kiely, Editor of *Marketing Magazine*

Jack Collis' enthusiasm and pragmatism make him one of the best speakers we have ever had.

Keryn Myers, Training Manager, Volvo

Jack Collis is by far the most remembered speaker from the conference. Never once in his two-hour presentation did his presentation lag or lose its excellence.

Paul Waite, General Manager, Mitre 10 Stores, Sydney

Real information, not just a show pony. He received a well-deserved standing ovation. At all times from lead-up to actual presentation Jack was a delight to work with.

Debbie Cameron, Principal,
Occasions Great and Small,
Brisbane

Jack, I was fortunate to attend one of your presentations to the Rural Press Conference at Yarrawonga. Yours was one of the most impressive presentations I have ever attended. Thank you.

Allan Hall, Advertising Manager,
Stock and Land newspaper

I think your presentation to the Suburban Newspapers Association was the best I have heard in my 30 years in newspapers.

F.J. Ryan, General Manager, *Macarthur Advertiser*

Jack, I want you to know how thrilled I am to have been in the audience this morning to hear your presentation. Your talk was the lesson in excellence that every Australian individual and business must hear. The stories you told rang too true.

Jan Jones, Success Talks

You helped make our Annual Conference the best conference we have ever had. So often our people are motivated for a short time by the guest speaker and then it's back to the usual. For the first time ever they remember and are doing something about it.

Joe Langley, Managing Director, Electronic Enterprises

Jack, you were magnificent. Thank you.

Ron Povey, National Sales Manager,
Friends Provident Life Office

Innovate

or
Die

Business thinking outside the square

Jack Collis

■ HarperCollins*Publishers*

HarperBusiness
An imprint of HarperCollins*Publishers*

First published in Australia in 2007
by HarperCollins*Publishers* Australia Pty Limited
ACN 009 913 517

HarperCollins*Publishers*
25 Ryde Road, Pymble, Sydney, NSW 2073, Australia
31 View Road, Glenfield, Auckland 10, New Zealand
77–85 Fulham Palace Road, London W6 8JB, United Kingdom
2 Bloor Street East, 20th floor, Toronto, Ontario M4W 1A8, Canada
10 East 53rd Street, New York NY 10032, USA

National Library of Australia Cataloguing-in-Publication data:

Collis, Jack.
   Innovate or die: Business thinking outside the square
   ISBN 13: 978 0 7322 8506 7
   ISBN 10: 0 7322 8506 2
   1. Success in business. 2. Creative ability in business. I. Title.
650.1

Typeset in Goudy 10/12 by Helen Beard, ECJ Australia Pty Limited

Contents

Introduction

How I became a speaker/presenter

In order to become an outstandingly successful speaker/presenter we first need to train ourselves in understanding the psychology of human beings and become expert in business techniques, because of all the presentations made by speakers, the great majority are made on those two subjects.

Speakers who want to make outstanding presentations need to have an excellent understanding of what humans do and how they feel, because when we make a presentation there will always be times when the audience asks, 'Why should we do what you propose?' or wants more information or further explanation. Presentations are strictly about the audience: how they feel and what they want to know. To be able to answer their questions to their satisfaction the speaker really does have to know the subject. Unless you are believable — and you won't be if you do not have a background of personal success in the subject you are presenting — your chances are minimal.

My training in this area began when I was about 10. Both my mother and father were avid readers, mostly of fiction and because we were a close family we talked a lot about the books we were reading. My parents often gave me their books to read and would ask me questions about the characters: what did I think of the main character? Did I agree with what the character had done in a particular situation? Would I have done things a different way if it had been me in that situation? From an early age I was subject to both male and female points of view, through both the characters in the stories and the views of my mother and father. I was also being trained in how to present my own viewpoint on how to deal with conflicting opinions: I had to learn and appreciate other people's points of view. There are very few cases where one point of view is the absolute truth.

What my parent taught me about life has stood me in great stead, especially in a career in business, which after all is only about people and their human strengths and weaknesses in a business environment. They are not business people, they are people who work in a business environment. Once we remember that it is their human viewpoint we are dealing with; we will seek human responses to issues and problems. I do not claim to be expert in either the male or female points of view but I do claim to have a better than average understanding of the psychology of human beings.

The knowledge I gained about people and how they feel and what they believe was a wonderful grounding for me during my school years. At that early age I was also learning the value of self-discipline. I soon learned that I needed good preparation and above all the discipline to do whatever was necessary to achieve my desired outcomes. As a child on early-morning errands I would time myself on the run home and every day tried to beat my best time. The discipline necessary to do this soon became a habit and beating my own best performance has stayed with me for a lifetime.

Success in life comes from managing ourselves in a competitive way, always believing that we can better our previous best performance. My father was a champion professional runner, football coach and a very good tennis player so his sporting background was in winning whenever possible. I was always involved in sport in my early years so the desire to be as good as I could, whether in sport or business, has always been with me and continued right through my business career. Life doesn't always produce wins so learning from losing was as important as winning. I have never seen losing as a problem, but rather as a need to re-evaluate what I had attempted and try again.

After finishing school I became an apprentice tailor, leaving home at 16 to continue my apprenticeship in Griffith, a large and prosperous town in the Murrumbidgee Irrigation Area of New South Wales. Two years later I joined the air force, serving for three years before marrying and buying a half-share in the business in which I had been an apprentice. Two years later my wife and I moved to Temora and started our own business, which we ran for 18 years until I joined AMP as a salesman.

I had only been in the business of selling insurance for about four months when I was invited to attend my first regional conference. The conference had been in progress for about two hours and the next item on the agenda was to be from a keynote speaker from our own ranks, a very successful senior agent.

About thirty minutes before he was to make his presentation I received a note from the divisional sales manager who was in charge of the conference. The note said, 'Jack, the main speaker has become ill and is unable to attend. I want you to take his place: speak on any subject you wish. You have one hour. Good luck.' Fortunately, I was a very organised agent and for the next hour my presentation was about the way I had structured my agency, how it worked and the success that it had brought me.

As a result of that presentation I was invited to become the keynote speaker at the New South Wales AMP representatives' annual conference held in Sydney at AMP headquarters. That address was also very successful and for the next two years I was the keynote speaker at that conference. From then on throughout my AMP career I was a regular speaker at their conferences, seminars and workshops. Three years later I entered AMP management as a Unit Sales Manager, responsible for recruiting, training and developing salespeople. Twelve years later after being a Divisional Sales Manager, Sales Manager for Queensland and Sales Manager for NSW, I became the AMP's first Marketing Manager.

I had always had an interest in organising and running various activities in sport, and when I went into business for myself I became a member of various business organisations, either as secretary, president, or some other office-holder. I joined Rostrum to learn more about public speaking and when I commenced my career in AMP this experience was of great value to me. Adding the training and development of salespeople to my skills was also very useful, for now I was developing and honing my understanding of human behaviour. I quickly learned why some people became great successes while others simply withered away. I learned what motivated people and what turned them off. I also learned the value of expressing ideas and communicating with my audiences in an original way. Throughout my career at AMP I was learning about business and the language of success and how to communicate it to other people and so I earned the reputation of being a great motivator. As my reputation in this area grew, other organisations began to approach AMP to have me speak at their conferences. This was agreed, as it was good public relations for AMP. Eventually, I approached a speakers' bureau to represent me. The demand for my speaking services became so big I had to make a choice between a career as a speaker or staying at AMP. My decision was to join the speakers' circuit and I resigned from AMP to become a full-time speaker/presenter.

Why this book?

While selecting the contents of this book it occurred to me that the book in its finished format would literally be the answer to the training, development and motivational needs of many organisations. Whether training is to be one on one, or delivered in a meeting format, every one of the presentations offered here will be very useful. The book could also be given to an individual as their own training program. They could select any chapter at any time and imagine that I am making a presentation personally to them.

It will be one of the most important and effective self-development books for those wanting to make progress in whatever field they currently work in. Why? Because it is a book for the times. In almost every presentation I have made, the issue is mostly about how well we are doing in the present and how well we are prepared to harvest the future. There is no future in the past, yet there are millions of humans at all levels in almost every type of organisation who are clinging to the past instead of developing themselves for the future. Why is this so? It is because we know how to deal with the past; that is where we have been living and working. The future is a question mark, yet already many are under pressure to define and deal with it. This book should be read by all who want to know how to best position themselves for the future they are going to live and work in for the rest of their working life. There is not a moment to waste.

I have spent 16 years on the international speaking circuit, during which time I have given over 1000 presentations on a great number of different topics to audiences ranging from Year 12 students to senior executives in all kinds of occupations and market segments. I have launched a variety of products and services including cars, health products, management systems, training methods, investment products and real estate. My presentations have covered selling techniques, marketing methods, management methods such as training and selection of key people and almost every other management discipline you can identify. These presentations were made in a variety of formats. Some were in workshop mode, some were in question-and-answer format. Most were delivered as presentations to audiences numbering from 20 to 900, with one audience of 4000. The duration of the presentations ranged from one hour to all-day sessions, and even to three-day workshops covering a variety of topics.

The overall objectives of the organisations I worked for were that the subject matter should be interesting, motivational, at all times realistic in terms of being possible and yet at the same time challenging, exciting and desirable. My comments should be future-oriented. How I dealt with their objectives was left entirely to me. The fact that I have been retained by a large number of organisations to be their keynote speaker and have made as many as 20 presentations to several organisations shows that I met their objectives.

It has always been my personal aim as a presenter to use descriptive words and phrases in a manner that will make my message memorable. If a speaker simply goes through the session without achieving this, they and their message will not be remembered for long and therefore will be less than effective. At all times when making a presentation the speaker needs to privately acknowledge that their audience may well have a lot of other issues on their minds and that, for many, the least important matter is the session they are about to listen to. Unless the presentation is well above the ordinary — and by that I mean challenging and motivational and presented in a way that literally demands to be listened to because it is perceived as being valuable — the audience may be there in person but absent in mind. The personality of the speaker must be built into the presentation in a way that attracts and holds the attention of the audience. Each member of the audience must have the feeling that the speaker is talking directly to them. Is all this easy? No it isn't. It takes a lot of hard work to achieve these aims and still leave the audience thinking the presentation was natural and easy.

Words are the children of our minds

Our thoughts are pictures in our mind and when they are vividly imagined they become very real to us. If we want to convey our thoughts to someone, or to an audience at a meeting or conference, it is necessary to convert our thoughts into words that can be understood by whomever we want to communicate with. Sometimes this requires a great deal of skill; not only must we convey the actual words, but we also have to ensure those words convey the meaning of our thoughts in a way that will also have meaning for our audience.

Words have great power: they can reduce people to tears, or make them joyous with laughter. They can build expectations, or destroy hope, or rally a nation. They can confirm an idea of great value, or move an organisation in a different direction. They can describe a new product in such a way that it determines the degree of its success in the marketplace. Whatever the situation, the more action implied by the words the more successful the announcement will be. Words are the children of our minds so be careful how you give birth to them. When they are born give them life by using expressive words that convey action, building their worth in the minds of those with whom you are communicating. If you do all this your message will be remembered long after you have given it.

The reason I believe this book will be valuable is because technology is currently ruling the roost and technology is cold and non-human; it has no warmth, no feeling. It is just a tool to be used and it is a poor communicative tool because it only reflects what the user puts into it, adding nothing itself. In the process of using technology the user has to give it a heart. I believe that the presentations in this book do exactly that.

Lastly, it is important that you, the reader, are aware that some key issues are repeated in a number of the presentations that make up this book. They are repeated because they are important and relevant to many of the wide-ranging topics covered in the book. For example, in the opening comments of many of my presentations, I describe the current situation in terms of the changes that are affecting business organisations and the lives of those employed in them. The changes taking place are common to all organisations, hence I use the same explanation in more than one presentation.

I wish you well in whatever enterprise you enter into, and remember, in the present business climate it is innovate or die. If you are not being innovative as a way of business life, then you are going to have a difficult time. If you are not being innovative in your own self-development you will have a difficult time. Ideas are money in the bank, and it could be your bank. So go for it with every skill you can muster. Remember, there is no future in the past.

1. Innovate or Die

The following half-day workshop presentation has been made to a large number of organisations, generally made up of individuals who were already very successful, but whose employers had realised that staying ahead in terms of personal development is never finished, or the business will die. Every year brings new and different challenges, for the world of business is getting ever more competitive, and each of us must meet the challenges or fall behind. The key to our past and future success has been and is the ability to be an innovative thinker, because today it is 'Innovate or Die'.

Mr Chairman, thank you for the kind welcome to your conference and for your invitation to make this presentation to you this afternoon. Let me begin by saying, as I do in all my talks, that some people die at 30 but are not buried till 70. Here lies the mind of an individual who at whatever age has stopped thinking, is mentally dead and just waiting to be buried. I know this does not apply to many, if any of you who are present today, but it serves to remind us that it is very easy to fall victim to the fallacy that we can now take it easy because we have done so well. Let me remind you that school is never over for those who want to survive and prosper in this new and different marketplace. There is no future in the past.

Today the rapid and constant change that is taking place in the world is causing concern to a great number of people. They worry about keeping up and wait in vain for yesterday to come back. The future is ahead of us and it is where we are going to spend our life. Day by day the future becomes today and we must not only work in it but our future depends on how well we continue to upgrade our skills. That means we must develop ourselves to match the needs of the day or fall behind. The fact of life is that most of us can take part in personal development. We do not have to stay at one level of ability forever. If we want more in terms of income or responsibility we can develop ourselves until we reach a level with which we are satisfied. The only real barriers to self-development are within ourselves. We can, if we choose, overcome any disadvantage to raise our standard of living and success in life. Will it be easy? For some it will. For many it will be difficult, but impossible for very few. I know this can be done because I have done it. I do not make this statement lightly. I know it will not be easy for many because life is not easy. Life is often difficult but it is rarely impossible for most of us.

Remember today it is innovate or die

We are living in the information revolution; you either join it or it runs over you — or worse still, it passes you by. Life is like an ice cream cone: you either lick it, or it drips on your shoes. What will be the biggest obstacle to our self-development, to making these changes? The answer, of course, is our thinking. Our greatest obstacle will be our business paradigm, which causes us to see our business future as an extension of today and restricts our ability to be innovative. A paradigm is a way of seeing the world as we believe it is. It could be said it is a set of rules and regulations. Boundaries that we have accepted and which, if adhered to, will bring us success. It is the way we do, or respond to, issues. It is the way we see our world. A paradigm could be a theory, a pattern, methods, protocols. Paradigms are the dominant patterns and mind-sets that make up our world, both in business and in our personal lives.

An understanding of paradigms is critical to our future, for two reasons. First, we will be faced with an ever increasing rate of change for the rest of our life and unless we can see the world with new eyes, we may miss our chance. Second, if we are to perform a positive role in the future, we will need to become our own futurists. We need to become innovators. If we try to solve today's problems with yesterday's solutions we will seek the future by looking through yesterday's eyes. We will become today-oriented instead of innovative and future-oriented. Remember, whatever you are doing and however you are doing it today, you need to accept that it is currently the most effective obsolete way available. You need to find a new and more effective way of progressing in this new and very different world. Today, as always, we see paradigms restricting progress in almost every industry and unless we look to new and radically different solutions we will become victims of our own paradigms. The only insight yesterday can offer is the opportunity to see what we must move away from. No industry is immune. Today it is innovate or die. We must break out of the restrictions of our own paradigms or become the victims of our inability to move forward into the new and exciting world that is waiting for us.

Ideas and innovation are the currency of today. In these changing times creative thinking is a necessity. Yesterday's solutions will not solve the problems of our new world. We are living in uncharted territory and we need to move beyond yesterday's world and look with fresh eyes to a new and different future. We can start by acknowledging that what we presently do not know is probably what we need to know. Does that mean that we have to forget all we know and start again? No it doesn't; that would be a catastrophe. What it means is that there are ways that are outside our present paradigms. It is our paradigms that limit our vision and stop us from becoming innovative. We tend to deal with issues we are familiar with and discount the new. But creative solutions and new ideas can be found in the smallest to the largest organisations. *Remember, the idea you have and don't use will be no more effective than the idea you have never had and can't use.* This is not a suggestion that you should go out willy nilly and try to implement every new idea you find. There must be investigation, inspection and critical analysis of whether your time and money will be well spent by running with a particular idea.

What is most likely to assist us in moving out of our present ways of thinking into methods that will ensure our success in this new and different world? The answer is self-development.

Self-development is essential if we are to move forward

Apart from increasing our income, self-development is a reward in itself. Once we taste the first success we open ourselves to the realisation that success at any level is full of the joy that comes with understanding we are in charge of our own self-development. Virtually anything is possible if we want it enough. Remember, there is no future in the past; today it is innovate or die.

In this presentation I want to focus on issues that are important to every person, no matter what they want to achieve in their life. If you are not effective in them your success in life will be limited. That doesn't mean you will not succeed, it simply means that when you set a limit to your personal effectiveness, you stay at that level. These issues are critical to achieving outstanding success in your life.

Success strategy for the individual begins with accepting that knowledge is the currency of today. It is money in the bank and it could be your bank. If you want to increase the value of your knowledge then you must constantly update and extend it so that you become a more marketable and valuable knowledge worker. Each of us has the capacity to increase our value by increasing our knowledge and skills. In this new 'knowledge society' it is the best available way. The greater your knowledge, the better your chances, provided you know how to make this new knowledge productive.

We need to predict a prosperous, happy and successful future, instead of the opposite. We need to tackle achievable, realistic goals so that we have no excuse for failing to try. We need to make sure that our self-talk —

about ourselves and others — is always positive. We need to give up being too critical. We need to eliminate negative self-talk. We need to apply the phrases *I can, I will, I want* as positive messages reinforcing the image we are trying to build. Last but not least, we should take responsibility for who we are and what we do. It is so easy to blame others for what is happening to us when in reality we are the architects of our own circumstances. When things go wrong, or right, they are generally of our own making. Self-image is the main factor limiting our level of performance and if we want to improve our performance we must first raise our self-image. To do this we should think positive, think success, read about success, talk success and mix with successful people and deny the unhappy negative people of this world. If we do only this we have a great chance of not only improving our self-image but of also achieving our personal and business goals.

Matching our performance against the characteristics of high achievers

To become a successful high achiever we need to learn how to achieve effectiveness in everything we do. We need to ask questions about the effectiveness and the characteristics of high achievers, questions such as: is getting things done simply a matter of personality? Or are drive, decisiveness, leadership and ambition the critical characteristics we need to attain? If we haven't got these characteristics, is there anything we can do about it? And to what extent is an ability to make things happen a matter of using techniques which can be learned and developed?

The first step is to accept that effectiveness can be learned. Personality is important — unless there is willpower and drive, nothing will get done. But remember that personality is a function of both nature and nurture. We are born with certain characteristics but upbringing, education, training, and, above all, experience develop each of us into the person we are. We can build on our own experience by observing and analysing the behaviour of high achievers, by understanding what makes them tick and then observing the personality characteristics and behaviours they display in getting things done. Observe what they do, how they operate, what techniques they use. Then analyse your own behaviour, (not personality) and compare it with that of high achievers. Think through how to improve your effectiveness. Learn as much as you can about techniques that will help you reach your success goals. Then match yourselves to the observable traits of high achievers.

Characteristics of high achievers

According to David McClelland of Harvard University, the characteristics of high achievers are that:

- High achievers set themselves realistic, achievable goals which test their ability and when achieved, ensure they have grown as a result.
- They prefer situations that they can influence rather than those over which chance plays a large part.
- They are concerned more with knowing what they have done well than with the rewards that success brings.

- They get their rewards from their accomplishments, ahead of money or praise. They do not reject money or praise as long as these are seen as realistic measures of their performance.
- They are most effective in situations where they are allowed to get ahead by their own efforts.

The fallacy of trying

If we want to succeed in life we need to give up trying. I don't mean give up attempting. The difference between trying and attempting seems to be that we ignore the truth of any attempt. The truth is that we either fail, or we succeed. Yet many simply say, 'I tried' as if that absolves them from the reality of failure and precludes any future action to achieve the same goal. Failure is not always 100 per cent; sometimes we might get 50 per cent of what we planned, or we might have made 90 per cent of what we planned. In both cases we are better off than before we made the attempt, but the truth is that we grow stronger if we accept that when we set a goal we either succeed and get the goal, or we fail. When we start thinking this way we increase our chances of success dramatically because we no longer use 'I tried' as an explanation or excuse for not having achieved the goal. I know it is only our choice of words, but words have great power and 'tried' seems to be used more to absolve us from succeeding than as a genuine explanation of what we did.

It is true that it is better to have tried and failed than not to have tried at all. But most of us have been brought up to view 'failure' as a word that has demeaning personal connotations. 'Tried' would not be a problem if we could see failure simply as it is; that is, 'I didn't get the goal 100 per cent'. The real problem is the accepted meaning of the word 'try'. Take athletics, for example: for years the greatest athletes in the world tried to break the four-minute mile barrier. For years they all failed to do it. One by one they made their attempts and failed, until the day Roger Bannister became the first man in the world to run the mile in under four minutes in a competitive race. Once Roger did it, the rest who had been 'trying' joined the under-four-minute club, because they now knew the four-minute mile was achievable.

Do we always succeed in achieving our goals? Or do we generally have to make more than one attempt? The truth is that many goals are not achieved at the first attempt. We make our first attempt and if we do not succeed we evaluate what we did and make a decision to change some elements of our plan and then make another attempt. We do that until we are forced to accept that we have failed, or we have succeeded. No matter what we are attempting in life, our success will be decided by our attitude. If we have a 'never say die' attitude, we are the possessor of one of life's great motivational and success factors.

Attitude is generally what separates winners from losers. Life is made up of winning and losing. It is rarely a case of always winning or always losing. The real issue is what we learn from winning and losing so that we can increase the wins and restrict the losses. How we react to winning and losing is a critical issue in building success in our life. In the end it is about how well we embrace self-development in our lives.

How you can and why you should develop yourselves

- Self-development will increase your knowledge and earnings and provide extra funds to grow your wealth.
- Get the list of issues that will help you develop yourself (it's in Chapter 5: 'You'll earn a fortune'). Choose from the list those ideas that you will employ to help you increase your ability — and do them.
- Your chances of building a better life depend on your ability to identify what you need to do and then to do it. *Start now*.
- Developing yourselves is the most cost-effective way of building your success and increasing your worth. When you are worth more to an employer you will be paid more.
- Never forget that in creating wealth in your life, developing yourselves is the one factor over which you have the most control and which can be done for very little financial cost.
- Every time you improve your ability you improve your financial worth to an employer, or increase your chances of becoming self-employed.
- Remember, no matter what your level of achievement, there is no stopping. As soon as we reach a desired level there is a tendency to breathe a sigh of relief and call time out, only to discover the winning post has moved again. The need for self-improvement is never finished because the world is moving on. We need to understand that self-improvement is a constant. If we stop at some level it

will not be long before we realise that what we are doing is the best most obsolete way currently available to us and now we must play catch up.

To increase our ability to innovate we need to rid ourselves of paradigms

To increase your level of success you need to become a paradigm breaker. Increase your creative thinking to unlock ideas that will create success in your life. The ability to understand paradigms is critical to our success, because unless we understand how to deal effectively with them we will be limiting our ability to create new ground-breaking ideas that can take us into the future. Remember, there is no future in the past and today it is innovate or die. At this stage I don't want you to think of all the reasons things can't be done, or why you will not want to do what is necessary. I want you to focus only on what you would have to do to get your goals. It is possible, no matter what the sceptics say. When humans are faced with a new challenge, in most cases their first thoughts are about why it can't be done; they think of all the reasons they may not want to do what needs to be done, because it will alter something in their life. This is natural. Humans tend to see tomorrow like today forever and as a result they do not like change. For instance, for the sake of this exercise let's suspend judgement on whether you want to do what needs to be done to become an outstandingly successful individual. Instead, let's focus only on what you can do to get that objective, then you decide whether you want to do it. Is that okay?

Paradigms are our mind-sets

Paradigms stop us from seeing opportunities. They cause us to resist change and live in yesterday instead of seeking the future with new eyes. Once you become a paradigm breaker you see with new eyes, opportunities emerge in a way that once seemed impossible and a new world of possibilities and opportunity limited only by your imagination is at your fingertips.

One paradigm we must break is the belief that the answers to our problems and opportunities lie within our own industry boundaries. We tend to only consider ideas and issues that are specific to our own industry. We give away the opportunity to be innovative when we don't learn to adopt and adapt ideas from industries outside our paradigm boundaries. Many of these industries have already solved our present problems. Why not learn from them?

Paradigms are a boundary outside of which we do not think

That's why thinking within paradigms restricts innovation and ideas. When new opportunities occur outside our paradigms we do not see them and therefore cannot take advantage of them. It is critical for our success that we take the time and effort to get the right answers before we discover we are living in the past. *If it's not broke, don't fix it* has been good advice for generations, but today if it's not broke, you're not looking.

Obstacles that hold us back and limit thinking creatively

Decide today and start to look with fresh eyes at the problems you need to solve to ensure your success. It is finally time to acknowledge that you can have the best-organised workplace in your business — perfect filing systems, etc., etc. — but if you are not firing at the high-priority objectives that will carry both you and the business forward to greater success, it may all be in vain. Go forward with every skill at your disposal; the world is waiting for you to claim your achievements. Get rid of the paradigms that are holding you back and join the innovative, thinking creatively brigade. Remember, ideas are the currency of today — money in the bank. Why not in your bank?

My comments are made to get you to embrace this particular way of thinking so that your perceptions are sharpened and you are always looking for the unexpected success, or failure, so that you can at least explore the possibilities of such successes and failures. Look outside your current paradigms and see the possibilities in a new and creative way. When you can consistently do that, your worth to the organisation in which you work will increase dramatically and when that happens your income should increase proportionately.

The positive outcomes of thinking creatively

Creativity has been increasingly seen as a process so rare in ordinary humans that it is a special gift, or level of genius, bestowed on the select few. This is simply not true. The truth is that our creative process is inhibited and constrained by several factors: our experiences at school, the influence of our parents in our formative years and, generally speaking, our desire to please and conform, lead many of us to become imitators rather than innovators. Once you focus on innovation you will see with new eyes. Ideas will flow to you once you break paradigms and reap the harvest of innovation. Will this be difficult? For some it will, but for most it won't. As the benefits flow from what you do, your confidence will grow, as will your reputation for creativity and innovation. Today ideas are money in the bank and it could easily be your bank. So go forward with confidence to the new and exciting future that awaits all those who embrace problems and ideas with confidence.

The new world of technology in which we must live

Suddenly we are being engulfed by change, not because we want it but because we have been resisting it for generations and now the floodgates are open and a new world is being born. The global village and the information society is now a reality. The growth of the information highway is visible evidence of this new information society and the major role it will play in our lives; the marriage of communications and computers has opened the world to anyone with the technology. Barriers that have stood for centuries have been smashed. Censorship is now almost impossible. The power base of many countries is being altered. Financial markets are at the mercy of the traders. Executive power is severely depleted, top managers no longer own the big picture, management layers have disappeared and it's a world in which communications and technology have rewritten the rule books.

As an example of technology making the past redundant let's take the typewriter. In the 1960s the typewriter was necessary equipment for almost every function in business and commerce. Along came the computer and the rest is history. The typewriter simply became a memory of how things used to be. This is happening in hundreds of different ways and will continue forever; another example is what is happening to fixed-line phones, which are rapidly being replaced by mobile phones. Technology will affect every one of us in some way.

Technology is driving the change. Our achievements in technology have now reached the point where many well-accepted beliefs have been overturned and replaced by new realities. There is no way of containing the technology explosion because creativity and innovation are the backbone of progress and mankind lives in an expanding universe so the law of expansion will prevail. The whole thrust of modern society is making it more necessary than ever to 'work smarter, not harder', and to play our part and share in the benefits of this new society we need to develop and constantly adapt our 'working smarter, not harder' skills to the changing demands of the workplace. More than anything else we need to focus on innovation as the most critical challenge that we and the organisations in which we work are facing because the old and familiar have reached their use-by date and we can no longer depend on past solutions to overcome today's and the future's problems.

More especially we need to constantly be innovative as time frames shorten and new and different solutions are needed.

The power of the customer is changing the way business sells its products and services and what products it produces and how. The customer has changed the way business competes and your customers will change the way you compete. Customers are the reason your organisation exists and they are your only source of profits. Any organisation which wants to succeed in today's customer-driven marketplace needs to become an advocate for the customer. Here are some of the questions to which you need to find short- and long-term answers because they are critical to your success.

Focus on the future of your organisation by asking

- What customers does the organisation serve now and how?
- Which customers will it serve in the future and why?
- Through what channels will it reach them and when?
- Who are its competitors?
- What is the organisation's competitive advantage and how can it use this to achieve its objectives?
- What skills or capabilities make the organisation unique and how will it use them to differentiate itself from others?
- What is it in our organisation that we should change and why?
- Are we focusing on innovation?

The critical issue for all organisations today is differentiation — how to make the organisation different in the perception of its customers — because it is that difference that draws customers. Your organisation's products, or similar products, can in most cases be obtained from an increasing number of alternative sources and as a result differentiation is critical to your future. The age and power of the individual has arrived as never before in our history. Intellectual capacity is our individual bank, our right to work, our passport to financial freedom. Ideas now drive organisations and ideas are the brainchild of the individual. And remember ideas don't care what sort of idiot gets them — so don't judge ideas by who gets them. The customer is king and the customer is an individual.

Innovate or die

We forget that jobs as we know them were created to fuel the Industrial Revolution. Until then, work was a cottage industry. People worked for as long as it took to provide what they needed. Then came the factories, and the mines to provide the power for the factories. Jobs were born because structured work was necessary; it was one of the greatest social upheavals in our history. Today, technology is causing the reverse to happen. It will be another major social upheaval, one that you will need to take account of. Jobs are becoming too structured to provide the flexibility needed by industry and commerce and so the move in many cases is back to work on a contractual basis. This movement to work, not jobs, will create opportunities in abundance for those who understand what is happening and who are willing to embrace work instead of jobs. The history of work is one of expansion driven by technology and it will not stop in the future.

When Henry Ford invented his car it was considered a useless invention: there were few suitable roads for mass use, too few people able to afford a car and all the usual reasons why it would not be a success were put forward. Those views were a product of the thinking of the day, which saw the future as an extension of the times instead of a new and different tomorrow.

Instead of the failure predicted, a nation built a system of roads that guaranteed the future of the car. Cars became trucks and shifted the produce of a nation. The car caused the world to change its shopping habits; new shopping centres grew in every part of the developed world. New holiday facilities emerged as people were able to travel according to personal desire. The motel industry was born to support travellers and the food industry played its part in the growth of economies, all of these developments producing work on a scale few could imagine at that time and I have only given one example of how technology and innovation drives an economy and produces work in abundance. All Henry Ford did was to free up travel for the individual. Perhaps we should be asking how we can free up whatever it is that we do.

I cannot remember another time when leadership in all sections of the community has been so desperately needed; leadership in terms of the acceptance by all kinds of organisations that the only real resource they have is the intellectual capacity of the people who make up their organisation. In whatever capacity we are involved as a leader, our role is to help those who work with and for us to achieve their true potential in terms of intellectual capacity. We are reaching a time in our development when the success of whatever organisation we are in will be decided by the intellectual capacity of its people. As the Society of Certified Practising Accounts (CPA Australia) has been telling us, 'The only true asset any business has is its human resource'. Each of us as individuals make up the organisation in which we work. Money, buildings, machinery and other non-human assets don't think. Only humans solve problems, design winning products, write creative profit-building advertising, recruit, teach, motivate, inspire and develop the potential of other humans, solve the problems and take advantage of the opportunities. Everything other than the human resource in an organisation is only organised rubble and one day it will return to rubble.

One of life's most special skills is innovative thinking — the ability to identify or create opportunities that others do not always see, to find solutions that turn problems into opportunities and to become a paradigm breaker. Once we master and adopt these techniques we will have greatly enhanced our ability to become an innovative and creative thinker. Remember, ideas are the currency of today's business world and of life itself. Ideas are money in the bank and it could be your bank.

If we are to make progress in terms of becoming more creative we need to explore and define more accurately the *how* and the *what* of creativity. We need to lay to rest some of the current accepted notions of creativity which in truth are only passed on untested. These are all too often wrongly accepted as facts and, if unchallenged, restrict our ability to be creative. Creativity and innovation have been increasingly seen as rare and special gifts. Sadly, the reality is that most of us lose our creativity once we grow up. During childhood we are essentially learning how to be human and as children we are forever asking 'why' and 'how' and 'what if'. As we mature, unfortunately we lose not the 'ability' to challenge current assumptions, but the 'desire' to challenge them. As we grow up we learn habits and fears that create blocks to being creative. Our social and work systems encourage conformity rather than the overthrowing of current methodologies to achieve better and swifter results. Most creative thinking and innovation comes about because of consistent hard work and a constant and passionate search for ways to grow the new and different, at the expense of the old and dying worn-out innovations.

Change is a constant in our lives, and creativity and innovation come about through the need for change. As humans and organisations we are facing a rate of change we have never experienced before. The need to adapt and move on is an issue for all humans. We live in an expanding universe and life itself is a continually expanding experience for all of us. Those of us who are willing can learn to be innovative and as a result grow and expand our careers and our lives.

Thinking creatively does not require genius; it only requires a questioning technique and a willingness to explore and reappraise established beliefs and positions. There are no absolutes except those of our own making. We need constantly to be aware that creativity requires us to do our own dismantling of established beliefs and positions. Creativity requires the constant use of both the left and right sides of the brain.

How to become an innovative thinker

Give yourselves a reason for creating new ideas

Why create ideas? Because you and the organisation in which you work need them to prosper and grow, and by creating them you build your reputation and your career. It may mean a promotion, a rise in salary — above all, it is the satisfaction of performing well, of achieving your goals and your potential as a human being. If you are self-employed in your own business, it is critical to your chances of success that you are constantly developing new ideas.

Think visually

Use the right side of your brain because it is your creator side. We are far more creative when we think in pictures. Nothing can be done until we first see what we want to do as a picture in our mind's eye. The more vividly we see it, the more certain it will become real in our life. We can do this through visualisation and affirmations. Close your eyes and relax and then build your idea in your imagination. Focus on it until it burns brightly in your mind and then affirm that it will become a reality in your life.

Focus on one idea at a time

Give your idea all your attention. Start with the big picture and then add or take away the detail a piece at a time until you have the finished picture in your mind. Then comes the left-brain thinking, the analytical approach. Keep adding the logical parts to your picture until your idea is complete and ready for you to test in the environment in which it is to be used.

Questions that create ideas

What can be added? Think of how vehicle manufacturers add to the features of last year's model to enhance its appeal and create more buyer desire for this year's model. *What can be taken away?* Think how often a product or a service is enhanced by removing a feature that didn't get the buyers' approval in terms of increased sales.

What else can be adapted? Developers of first homes for new buyers in the USA found their product was only receiving lukewarm acceptance because, although the price was right, buyers knew they would soon grow out of the house as children arrived in the family and they were worried about resale values. The developers made two key options available to buyers:

1. They redesigned the house and sold it as it currently was but with an option to add a well-planned addition that would take care of the increased size of the family when and if it became necessary.
2. They wrote into the agreement of sale a buyback option guaranteeing that they, the developers, would buy back the house from the purchasers at an agreed price when and if they wished to sell. Result: immediate buyer response. The developers had in fact created a new industry segment simply by asking how they could adapt the original house to suit first home buyers and their needs as their family grew. That's thinking creatively.

Is there something that can be duplicated? Some nations have built their prosperity by manufacturing products innovated by other nations — sometimes even selling them back to the nation whose product they have copied. Franchising was duplicated worldwide by all kinds of businesses making and selling all kinds of merchandise and services. As an example of imitators, General Motors got into automobiles by way of imitation, as did most other automobile manufacturers. The list of imitators is endless.

What can be included? One of the great creative ideas of all time came from Henry Ford. When he was building his model 'T' Ford, he outsourced the manufacturing of many of the car's components. The contract that the various suppliers had to sign included a clause stipulating that parts were to be delivered in a special kind of box. The clause specified that the box had to be made of a particular hardwood and there were to be a specified number of slabs which had to be fixed with a special sized counter-sunk screw. Even the location of the screw holes was indicated on the diagram which accompanied the contract.

The reason for all of this became obvious when the parts were delivered. As soon as the parts were taken out of the box, the box was taken apart and it and the screws were delivered to the assembly line where it became the floor of the model 'T' Ford. Simply brilliant — and an example of the power of thinking creatively.

Adding value: the power of the right question

The example I'll relate now is about a restaurant that added value in a different way. It was a Mexican restaurant and the problem was that the restaurant did very well on every day except Sunday. The owner realised that the Sunday day trade was not likely to take off, but he wanted to build the Sunday night trade. He sought my help as a marketing consultant and explained the problem he wanted to solve. I then asked the following questions: *Who are your main customers?* Answer: Americans. *Why Americans?* Answer: Because they love Mexican food. *Where do they live?* Answer: In the same general locality as the restaurant.

My solution was as follows: *If you find out what Americans like as much as, or even more than, Mexican food and you give it to them, they will fill your restaurant on Sunday nights.* The owner came back several days later and said to me that the answer to my question was gridiron football. That's what Americans like as much as, or even more than, Mexican food. So the restaurant owner sent a man to the US who met with the people who taped the gridiron match of the week. They said they would like to get exposure for the game in Australia and were willing to send him a tape each week. This enabled the restaurant owner to do a 5000-leaflet letterbox drop saying, 'If you come to our restaurant on Sunday night of this week you will receive an 8-course Mexican food banquet dinner at a special price and we will show you last week's gridiron football match, free of charge.' The result was the restaurant was filled on Sunday nights and 'Gridiron Sunday' became a stunning success.

The unexpected success or opportunity

This is the most underestimated opportunity in business. It is almost risk free, it generally occurs in all types of organisations and yet it is just as often overlooked or ignored. The classic example comes from the Swiss watch industry. Around 1967 the Swiss controlled the world watch market. At that time some of their key designers produced a new watch. It had no springs or winding mechanism, unlike the watch of the day. It was so different, the Swiss said it would be difficult to market. So sure were they of their opinion they put the watch on display at the World Convention, without patenting their design. Seiko of Japan and Texas Instruments saw it, took the idea and developed it and the rest is history. The Swiss lost an enormous opportunity. Thousands of watchmakers became unemployed. Who controls the watch industry today? Japan. What sort of watch? The Quartz watch, which most of us are wearing today. Why couldn't the Swiss see its potential? Because of their watchmakers' paradigm. The watch was too different. Too new. That's the reason so many great opportunities are ignored by so many different types of organisations. If we want to grow our skills, one of the most important is to develop our ability to *think creatively* and take advantage of asking the right questions.

The unexpected failure

The classic in this category is the Edsel car, developed and manufactured by the Ford Motor Company in 1957. Very few products of any kind have been better researched and manufactured than the Edsel car, yet from day one it was a failure in the marketplace. To their credit, Ford went back to the marketplace to find out what had gone wrong. They found the car was okay but the market segment they had built it for had moved on to lifestyle thinking and the car had arrived at the wrong time. Using this information, Ford produced the Thunderbird, which became the greatest success of any American car since Henry Ford built the model 'T' in 1908. They turned the unexpected failure into a wonderful opportunity and success.

Turning negatives into positives

When new ideas are proposed in the process of resolving a problem or instituting new procedures, people often respond negatively. In this exercise, try to turn these negative statements into positives. Write them down for future use.

- Don't be ridiculous! It costs too much! That's outside our area!
- We don't have time! It's not our problem! Let's get back to reality!
- You're ahead of your time! Has someone else tried it? It's too hard to sell!
- That will make other things out of date! You can't teach an old dog new tricks!
- Let's shelve it for the time being! It needs more market research!

Developing innovative thinking

Humans tend to see tomorrow as if it is today forever. But once you become an innovative thinker you see with new eyes; opportunities emerge in a way that once seemed impossible, a new world of possibilities limited only by your imagination and innovation is at your fingertips. One paradigm we must break is the belief that the answers to our problems and opportunities lie within our own industry, or occupation boundaries. We tend to only consider ideas and issues that are specific to us and we give away the opportunity of learning to adopt and adapt ideas from other sources outside our boundaries, many of those industries have already solved our present problems so why not learn from them?

Why do some people fail to innovate? Because of their unquestioning and deeply rooted beliefs in the way they do things, which stops them from seeing new opportunities. We are always seeing the world through the lens of 'how we do things' and 'what we stand for' — our rules and regulations tend to describe our paradigms. Corporate consultant Joel Barker has done a great deal of work on paradigms and authored a video on the subject. He says that the key question we should ask ourselves and others is, 'What is impossible to do now, but if it could be done, would fundamentally change our business or occupation?' He says that this question forces each of us to identify and deal with innovation.

Some illustrations of innovative thinking

Have you ever received a package, or parcel delivered by a courier? Have you noticed that when the item is delivered, you sign for it and then the courier is gone in a flash? Sometimes if the doorbell is not answered immediately the courier is gone by the time the door is answered, which is good. The item has been delivered on time. I admire the service, but wonder why the couriers don't ask for business. Perhaps it's not their responsibility and that's fair enough. But no one from the courier company rings and asks, 'Can we deliver for you? We would like you as a customer, can we do business?' It would be easy for the courier to ask, 'Anything to deliver now that I am here?' The reason they don't ask is because they are stuck in the courier paradigm. They see their business as delivering, not getting new business. But if they thought innovatively, it would be different.

More innovative questions and ideas

Is there something that I could offer to my customers that they may like enough to grow my business and increase my profits? The potential of this question is enormous. It could be a product or a service. It could be a new way of financing a purchase, or it could be an extended guarantee of a product or service liability. It could be a new way of differentiating your business from your competitors. It could be a buyback guarantee within a limited time. The possibilities are only limited by our imagination and our willingness to do it.

Here are two more great questions: *What is it that we currently can't do, but if we could, it would build our business and increase our profits?* And: *What are other businesses not in our field doing to grow their business and that, if we did the same, would grow our business?*

Here is another creative idea that is a paradigm breaker: let's imagine you want to make an offer by letter, to selected prospects, of a new and exciting product. You are at your desk and you have written the letter making the offer. How do you send it? In an envelope by post of course, that's how we send our letters, don't we? But we are going to break our 'post a letter' thinking — we are going to send our letter in a 'bottle'. Yes, a plastic Australia Post-approved bottle with an address label on one side and a small advertisement on the other. Similar postage rate to a letter. Which do you think will get the most attention? The bottle wins hands down. Why don't we think of using a bottle? Because our 'post a letter in an envelope' habit gets in the way. You want some bottles? Call The Ideas Machine in Brisbane.

Fears hold us back

Fears are the result of our own imagination, yet they are a constant inhibitor to our success. We humans are born with only two fears. They are the fear of loud noises and the fear of falling. All other fears are the result of our responses to life experiences. As long as we give in to them they can grow to become major obstacles and barriers to superior performance. The key to overcoming them is to confront them with desire, for if our desire is greater than our fear we will win.

Losers in life tend to focus on process. They fall in love with the methodology rather than results. They are more interested in a pleasing method. Winners focus on results. They will endure the pain of any method as long as they achieve a positive result and that is the habit we need to cultivate. The critical life skills of *goal-achieving*, *using your time effectively* and *becoming an innovative thinker* are sure-fire ways of increasing your effectiveness, achieving positive results, building your career and reaching your possible dream. Few if any of us can afford to follow the old straight road to the future because it is disappearing and we have to contend with a new and very different world. Our ability to become a winner in this new and different world will be decided by how willing we are to make the changes necessary to not only survive, but to succeed in whatever area of business and commerce we are in.

Ideas are everywhere

Ideas and innovation are the the currency of today. They are money in the bank and it's your money and your bank. In today's world, creative thinking is a necessity.

Many ideas that have been useful to me have come through the letterbox as what is usually described as 'junk mail'. This type of mail has many good features, one of which is that it has to get our attention, and in order to achieve that, someone spends a great deal of time and effort. They devise ways of getting it noticed, either by how it looks, or what it says and how it says it, or even how it is formatted or folded, or the sequence used to deliver its message. Recently in some junk mail I received a letter advising me of the address of a new business. Nothing unusual in that, except that when they gave their address they said, 'The GPO is next to us'. Now that will get noticed; it's a different way to get attention. Most people would have said, 'We are next to the GPO'. Why? Because they are smaller than the GPO.

The unexpected success

The unexpected success is the opportunity that too often goes unnoticed or ignored. Why? Because no one expected it to happen. I know because this happened to me when I produced a new way of accounting for and keeping track of the Training Guarantee Legislation (TGL) requirements which had to be met by most businesses some years ago. Previously, training costs could be claimed as tax deductions. No records of the training were required. The TGL dictated that special records be kept in a designated order to claim deductions. I saw this new product as a 'give away' to clients that retained me to do some of their training which came under the requirements of the TGL. After I had produced the package I mailed a number of businesses offering my services in sales training and detailing the package they would receive. Not everyone needed my services (many had their own training support) but they did require the TGL package and replied asking its cost as a stand-alone product. I put a reasonable price on the package and they bought it. I then advertised the package by direct mail and it became an outstanding seller, which also brought me many sales training assignments. So many times a business or individual is so focused on what is usual and what they expect that when the different, or unusual, or unexpected arises they take little or no notice and another opportunity goes begging.

Filenes of Boston – the greatest sale lottery in the world

When my wife and I were in Boston on business for AMP we were often asked if we had been to Filenes. We were asked so often we went to see what was so special about Filenes. It was a wonderful experience and a great example of creative thinking. Filenes is an upmarket, nine-storey shopping experience. High-class merchandise. They have a bargain basement in which they run the most creative sale I have seen. Seven days a week.

Here is the creative twist. I will use a men's suit as an example of what happens with all the merchandise in the bargain basement. Let's say I am interested in buying a good suit at a bargain price and I have gone to Filenes' bargain basement. Firstly, there are lots of suits — hundreds, all at sale prices. So what? Everyone has sales. But not like Filenes. The suit is prestige quality, normally selling for, say, US$4000. Attached to the cuff of the suit coat is a price tag that gives today's date and today's sales price of $3000. That's good value but you can get that offer in most stores. But there is more. Just below that price, there is a statement that says if it is still here in three days' time you can buy it for $2000. Below that price there is a statement that if it is still here in six days' time you can buy it for $1000. If it is still here in nine days' time you can buy it for $500. If it is still here in 12 days' time, it goes to charity.

My prices and time factors may not be exact because time dims memory, but they are correct in principle and a true example of the way the bargain basement functions. Filenes uses the most creative sales technique I have ever seen: a grand sale with a built-in lottery technique that has universal appeal. The day we were there we were amongst thousands. You should have seen some of the people trying to hide the merchandise to improve the price. This innovative sale 'lottery' technique was made possible because someone asked, 'How can we do it differently and increase our sales?' I suspect it was another unexpected success, probably invented to sell some sale merchandise, and it turned into a permanent sales winner. Question: how can you use ideas to make money for you and the organisation that you work for? Remember what Thomas Edison said:

> 'Make it a practice to keep on the lookout for novel and interesting ideas that others have used successfully. Your idea has to be original only in its adaptation to the problem you are working on.'

Questions are the answer to most innovative ideas

Here is another example of creative thinking. After I gave a presentation to around 200 small-business people on the topic of 'Ideas Unlimited', focusing on ideas that other businesses had used successfully, many participants had specific questions on particular aspects of my presentation. Among the questions was one by a young couple who said they manufactured garages. Their question was: 'Jack, we manufacture garages. We like your follow-up ideas, but we can't just write to someone three months after they have bought a garage and ask them to buy another one.' I had to agree, but asked them: 'What is a garage? Why do people buy them?' They replied, 'To put their car in them.' In other words you are really selling a storage system for a car. They agreed, but didn't think of it that way. What else do people store in their garage? The couple replied, 'Anything they can't store in the house.' Then I asked, 'How often do you write to your customers to sell them storage systems for all the other things they store in the garage?' They said that they never sold any storage systems because they didn't think of garages as storage systems, and they only manufactured and sold garages. Here is a perfect example of what Edison was saying.

Let's look at the potential extra sales to someone who has had their new garage for around six months, including winter. I had asked the business couple, 'When you sell a garage, how many of the buyers order an automatic door with their garage?' They said about 80 per cent. The other 20 per cent get a manual door. My suggestion to them was why not write to them after six months saying:

> *Dear customer, you must be tired of getting wet when it rains and you have to get out of your car to open the door! For 'X' dollars we can convert it to automatic and you can stay dry and comfortable in your car. Not only that but we can install build-to-measure storage for all those things you are constantly falling over, or can't find in your garage, call us on xxxxxxxx.*

If they don't answer, call them on the phone and make them an offer they can't refuse. These solutions are just another example of asking the right questions and then selling the solution.

Systematising an idea

What about franchising — the boom industry that has touched almost every other industry? It was a logical step up from the perfection of the production lines of manufacturing. Someone one day must have said, 'I know how to run this type of business. I have perfected the manufacturing, sales and marketing of this product. I have systems that work, buying power etc., etc., so I will sell my system and I will call it franchising.' Here was a creative solution based on intellectual property.

Can your business be franchised? Can part of it be franchised? Can you franchise yourselves? Of course you can: it's called coaching, or mentoring.

Asking the right questions can make you a fortune

Speaking of franchises, McDonald's was started when Ray Kroc noticed the unexpected success of one of his customers. Kroc was selling milkshake machines to hamburger businesses and he noticed one of his customers was buying more milkshake machines than his business could justify by size and location. When Kroc investigated this unexpected success, he found that the old man who owned the shop had reinvented the fast food business by systematising it. Kroc bought his business and it became the billion-dollar business we know as McDonald's. Thousands of customers must have bought from the old man's original business but none until Kroc had asked, 'Why is this business so successful?'

How to create a near-monopoly in small business

Here is another example of creative thinking to solve a problem. I was presenting to a seminar of around 125 small-business people, again on the topic of 'Ideas Unlimited'. At lunchtime the owner of the conference venue in which the seminar was held told me he had built the centre and accompanying restaurant specifically to cater for the conference and wedding reception and restaurant market. It was a first-class centre but it was located on hectares of gardens several kilometres from the town centre. The problem was that he was not attracting enough of the wedding reception market, which was substantially larger than the seminar–conference market.

Here is how he solved the problem. Firstly, he researched the wedding market in much greater detail than he had done originally and found that on average there were 14 different businesses involved: clothing, cars, photography, flowers, venues, travel, and many others. So he invited the owners of the principal business in each of the 14 categories to a lunch at his restaurant. At the lunch he suggested that if each of the businesses involved produced a value-for-money special package for weddings and all 14 of the businesses rolled their package into a total single offer, they would have a financial advantage that literally could not be beaten. The agreement was that whichever business received the first inquiry would then sell in the other 13 as a complete package. He told me that it was a great success and that he now had the major share of the business in his category.

How can you use this idea? Can you adapt it? Build on it? Whatever you can do may have the effect of creating more, or a different business. None of this innovation works until someone asks 'Why?'

You don't have to be big to get world-class ideas

As I said earlier, creative solutions and new ideas can be found in the smallest and the largest organisations. *Remember, the idea you have and don't use will be no more effective than the idea you have never had and can't use.* Step outside your current way of thinking and explore new and creative possibilities.

What you need to do to get the most from this chapter

Accept that ideas and innovation are the currency of today. Money in the bank. Be sure and get your share. The reason so many of us fail to make gains from our ideas is that our paradigms stop us from seeing the opportunities. Become an innovative thinker by always challenging your assumptions. Are they true, or just a habit of seeing issues as you have always seen them? Always ask *why*? Always ask *what if*? Then check to see if your *what if* would work. The unexpected is the opportunity that too often goes unnoticed. Look for the unexpected success or failure. Read again the examples in this chapter and ask yourself, 'What if I applied that concept to this situation?' Talk with people outside your industry and you will find many ideas you can adapt to your work. Stay alert. Watch junk mail for creative ideas. Implement some of them. Remember, the idea you have and don't use will be no more productive than the idea you never had and couldn't use. The way to test an idea is to do it on a small scale — and if it works, go for it. Read again the story of Ray Kroc and how he started McDonald's. Once you become ideas-oriented you will draw ideas to you and ideas don't care who gets them.

The question technique

Here is a list of questions, each of which has the power to create ideas that will help you to become innovative. Some of these questions we have already explored, but it's worth listing them again for further consideration:

- What can be added?
- What if it were exaggerated?
- What else can this be used for?
- What's being wasted that could be put to use?
- What else is like this?
- What else can be adapted?
- Is there something I can duplicate?
- How can this be done better and more cheaply?
- How can this be made more appealing?
- What can be substituted?
- What should be subtracted?
- Can it be done faster?
- What ideas can be combined?
- How can this be condensed?
- What's the opposite of this?
- What if nothing is done?
- How can we use changes in perception, in mood, in meaning?

The creativity gap

The creativity gap is a phrase used to focus attention on the need to keep practising skills that enhance creativity. These skills include:

1. Observing and paying close attention to events as they take place, or to the situation after events have taken place.
2. Memorising these observations in detail so you can recall them if necessary.
3. Analysing then judging your observations. Visualise the non-existent, which is another way of developing a positive constant habit which leads to creating solutions that currently may not exist.

The positive outcomes of being innovative

- You will become a paradigm breaker because you will accept that thinking within paradigms is the reason so few people are creative in their work.
- You will adopt a questioning technique towards your life events and your work and you will search for ways to make improvement in your life and your work.
- Ideas that will improve your life and work will come easily to you because you will seek them out, evaluate them without prior prejudice and implement those that pass your tests.
- You will become a *why not* person, challenging the old ways and implementing the new ways that lead to a more successful future.

- Your reputation as a creative person will grow and your views will be sought. You will be seen as a change-maker who grows your life and the business in which you work.
- Your focus will always be on being effective. On being results oriented. You will be willing to cut out the window-dressing and go for the winning result.

The search for new and better solutions that will grow and develop ourselves and our organisations is the number one priority of true leaders. In your endeavours to reach this goal do not let yourselves be deterred by those with less vision, a weaker commitment and a stronger desire to live in the present until it becomes the past. Today it's innovate or die. When you are told, 'Don't do it that way; it would be easier to do it this way,' remember that, as playwright Neil Simon said, if Michelangelo had taken that advice he would have painted the Sistine floor and his masterpiece would soon have been lost forever beneath the trudging feet of the people who look down in search of certainty and safety instead of up to the challenge of the future — which is innovate or die.

2. Building a Winning Sales Team

This presentation was made to a conference of suburban newspapers. I had been asked to give them information on what I would do to make a sales team run and become exceptional in terms of selling space in a newspaper. They had retained me because of my experience in selecting, training and motivating sales teams in the insurance industry. Following is the content of the address I made, at the conclusion of which the audience gave me a standing ovation. You can be a winner if you follow the ideas as they are written — exactly as they are written. Then implement the ideas that you are currently not using.

Mr Chairman, thank you for your kind welcome and introduction. It is my pleasure to share this conference with you and your people. My subject for this presentation is 'Building a Winning Sales Team'. I have been asked to briefly outline the training methods that I personally used to build my own team of salespeople. Let me begin the way I start most of my presentations. Some people die at 30, but aren't buried till 70. Here lies the mind of an individual who at the age of 30 has stopped thinking, is mentally dead and just waiting to be buried. I know this is not true of those who are here at this conference, but it is worth remembering it can happen to anyone, at any time, unless they stay ahead of changes affecting us almost every day.

Firstly, when we hire a salesperson, contrary to the popular belief that as long as you're alive and breathing you can get a position selling insurance, it is actually fairly difficult for any new recruit to get through the screening process that we use to select a new agent. Training an agent successfully costs a good deal of money and we are not anxious to spend that money unless we feel we have a better than average chance that the person we appoint will succeed in the business.

I have been asked to focus on those issues that in my opinion make a sales team perform above the ordinary. So let us assume that you have hired me to make your sales team run. Of course, I will not presume that you do not already know what I'm going to talk about, or that your sales team is not the best in the country. I am simply giving you my point of view. If you disagree, all I ask is that you don't throw anything heavy because I am getting slower on my feet these days.

Let's assume that you have put me in charge of developing a sales team for you and you have said that you want a top-performing team. High-performing sales teams in your business need to be highly motivated to sell print space.

Now that I have described Utopia to you, if I had any brains I would leave. But seeing as you have asked me here, I will do my best. From here on I am going to be working with each of you to build a high-performance sales team.

This is how I would go about building it; it is how I built my own team.

First of all, I will only hire successful people. This is a most difficult area so I will lay down some very simple criteria. I will only hire people who have been successful at what they have previously done. What I mean by that is that if tomorrow I am talking to a taxi-driver who wants to sell some space for us, provided he is in the top 20 per cent of the taxi-drivers who currently drive taxis in Sydney, then I will think about hiring him. If he has been a salesman then I want to know that he has a good track record because I am not going to hire people who do not have a good track record. If he is a schoolteacher who wants to sell space for me, unless he is a really good schoolteacher — in the top 20 per cent — he is not going to be on my team. This rule applies equally to males and females.

If there is anything I have learned in 22 years of constantly watching, helping, selecting, training and motivating salespeople, it is that leopards do not change their spots. The world is full of managers who seem to believe that, given the chance, they will change this or that person's characteristics. My answer to that is: bunkum. If he, or she, came to work late in their last job then after a while they will get to work late in this one. If they didn't like their last position the odds are they won't like this one. If they didn't succeed in their last job the odds are high that they won't succeed in this one. So in simple terms I am going to look for people with a salesperson's success characteristics. That is, they're healthy, have a good outgoing personality and can take a knock-back when it comes, as it surely will. They need to be success focused. Dependable and willing to learn. They need to be willing to work under instruction while learning the business. Unless they are successful at what they are currently doing they can't become part of my team. For the sake of simplicity, from here on whenever I say 'he' or 'him' you should assume the situation or example applies to both males and females.

I am going to describe the job accurately

I am going to tell them about the job, warts and all. Then I am going to find out their philosophy on life and how much they want to achieve. Then I am going to sell them my philosophy on life, which is very simple, by telling them, 'You can stuff up your life but I don't want you stuffing up mine. I only work with successful people. If you don't want to be a success, you can't be on my team. If you can't drive yourselves out of bed every morning to sell space for me because that is what you want there is no point in coming with me. If you don't want to be the best space seller in the whole business, if you don't want more than what you currently have, I don't want you to come with me.'

So let's assume that they have passed my test and that they accept my philosophy. The next thing I will do is to set minimum work effort performance standards. I am going to tell them that they can perform at this level and stay, but if they don't they will have to leave because I don't want to work with unsuccessful people. I will give them a reasonable goal and a reasonable minimum standard of work performance because, if there is anything I have learned about managing salespeople, it is that if you can get them to work you can teach them to sell. But if you get those who will not work it doesn't matter how well you teach them to sell. I am looking for a worker. I am looking for someone who feels compatible with me and I want to get him excited about what we're going to do together. I want him to understand that minimum performance standards are our aim and must be achieved or he cannot stay in my team.

When I have given this new salesperson minimum sales performance standards, then I will try to raise his standards until he becomes a superior performer. Remember, I said the real issue in performance standards is work. I am going to give them activity goals of how many people they should call on in a day, how many people they should ask for an order in a day, how much they are to sell in a week, how much space we have to sell, what the average size of a good advertisement is and how much a client will pay for it.

Then I am going to teach this new salesperson where to find the prospects they will need in order to be successful in selling space for me. Most salespeople leave the selling business because they can't find people to talk to. I am going to make sure that this new salesperson understands what makes a good prospect. People who have bought a business and want to change its name. People who have just gone into business and want to advertise their name. People who have just gone into business and want to tell the world they are in business. People who are having a sale and want to tell people, 'You can buy it better here.' There are so many reasons why people want to buy space. So I am going to teach this new salesperson how to prospect and the system he must follow. I'll show this new salesperson how to develop the best prospecting system; how to list them and give them priority, how to work on them. Then, when I am sure that he understands where to find the people with whom he is going to do business, I will teach him how to approach them.

The first part of making the approach is to prepare for knock-backs, to know in advance what it is you want to sell, why you want to sell it, who you want to sell it to and how much of it you want to sell. I need this new salesperson of mine to understand the top four reasons our prospect is going to say, 'I don't want to buy it'.

- I don't want to buy it because it is too expensive.
- I don't want to buy it because I don't believe in it.
- I don't want to buy it because I don't need it.
- I don't want to buy it because I haven't the money to pay for it.

Then I am going to teach this new recruit how to answer those objections because, if our salesperson isn't ready to sell, the prospect isn't ready to buy. I am not going to run a team of salespeople who just go around the traps picking up what they can. Don't misunderstand me: going around the traps and picking up the business that is there every week is an essential part of a good sales team. But maybe we can pick up a lot of that over the phone without very much eye contact and without very much effort at all, especially when we have built a good relationship with our prospect. What we want every week is to prove we are getting better at this job of selling. We want to prove that we are getting stronger at selling, that we are getting richer at this job. We want to be doing it better than anyone else. Why? Because we want to be excited about it and we want to get out of bed every morning anxious to get to work.

Nothing succeeds like success; the more you sell, the easier it is to sell. The more you want to sell, the easier it becomes to want to sell. It is a never-ending cycle that starts with someone wanting to do what they are paid to do — so I am going to have this new salesperson understand comprehensively this simple statement: *Mr Jones, the reason I have called to see you this morning is* . . . If he hasn't got one of our little cards noting the reason he is going to see Mr Jones and noting on the other side of the card the four objections Mr Jones is likely to raise and four first-class answers to those objections, then this salesperson is not ready to sell. If the salesperson is not ready to sell we don't want to waste time.

So we now have our salesperson there and making the approach. The key issue about making approaches is to be interesting. It is all about having a prospect willing to trade their time for our ideas. I will teach my salespeople that if they use an approach used by other salespeople, that has the same idea and the same tired old expressions other salespeople used in their approach, and our prospect has learned to say no to all the others, then they will get the same response as the others.

I am going to teach my new salesperson to be exciting. We need to be enthusiastic and we need to know why we are there and we need to have constructive ideas about how what we are offering will make life better, easier, and more profitable for our prospect. We are going to be interesting to talk to. This salesperson is going to be trained every day of his life to be interesting so that when he walks away, even if prospects don't buy, they will surely remember him. They should be left with the feeling, *I am glad I had the opportunity of listening to him today because I now know a lot more about things than I knew before* because in making our approach and in making sales our salesperson is going to understand they don't sell space, they sell a philosophy of life which is funded by the space they sell.

Every successful salesperson I have ever known didn't sell a product; they sold a philosophy of life and their skill was in the way they made the philosophy come alive. In our case, our new salespeople will sell a philosophy of life to their prospects: how to make their life more successful, how to get what they want from life. Space is only the means of funding it and providing the money to implement the philosophy. So when we talk to someone who wants to advertise a restaurant we want our salesperson to tell this restaurant owner what they can do to make their advertising work more successfully. To be successful our salesperson has to make his clients successful, or he will become a loser. He will by his own example and attitude to life expound the philosophy that we work in a great system, a free enterprise system, that it's a great country, a lucky country and if you want to be in it you can be. If the prospect wants to win, my salesperson is going to help them win and after he has talked to them for a while they are going to feel that they're going to win. The prospect will understand what winning is all about because this is the philosophy our salesperson will sell to his prospects. He's going to show people how to win more often, to win whatever it is they want out of life — whether it is more money, more travel, more time, more happiness, more success, more recognition, more pleasure, or more excitement.

The only reason they have to buy space is because it will help them fund what they want. Whatever they want, our salesperson is going to show them how to get it. Can you imagine that by this time they will not be interested in getting what they want? That's why they are in business. If they are not in business for those reasons, what reason is there to be in business? Winning salespeople get results because they don't sell a product, they sell what a product will do for their customers. Our salespeople will never be afraid to tell their prospects, 'I want you for a customer because I want to show you how to win.' Can you imagine a prospect saying, 'I don't want to win'?

I am going to teach my salesperson how to ask for orders and to understand that the salesperson who cannot ask cannot live. A salesperson who cannot ask for the order fails and therefore cannot make a living as a salesperson. The business of a salesperson is to sell. I am going to teach them that integrity, morality, honesty and ethics are the codes by which our sales team is going to live. No sharp practices, no conning people; we're going to tell it in an exciting way, we're going to tell it as it is. And then they are going to ask for the order. Many salespeople find it difficult to ask for the order, yet the easiest thing in the world is to simply say, 'What do I have to do to have you become my customer?' I will teach them the *not if but which* technique of closing a sale.

Then I will teach this salesperson of ours about servicing the customer, about analysing repeat business, about analysing what each customer is worth to him and to me.

About the real value of the customer. I will show him how to keep good sales records which will allow him to analyse his work so that he can do it more effectively than ever before. And I will never fail to tell him that he has done a good job — firstly for the client, secondly for himself and thirdly for me. I will acknowledge his contribution towards our overall goals. I will keep him informed about what we are trying to do and I will ask for his ideas so that he can contribute further. Then I will listen to what he tells me and whenever possible I will see that we implement some of his ideas.

All the while I will be teaching my salesperson a philosophy of life. As we progress I will be educating my team about how to get more out of life than they ever dreamed of. I will teach each member of my team how to do this and last but not least I will always treat my new sales team as important and valued human beings who sell space for me. I will never treat them as salespeople first and human beings last. I will always be interested in what each member of the sales team wants to achieve for themselves and their family and I will do my best to help them get what they want. I will teach my sales team how to set and get their life goals. All the time I will be working hard to have every member of my team grow as a person. To be better at selling and to want and get more from life. I will help them understand that they can have whatever it is they want if they know the rules of life — and if they don't, I will teach them the rules.

And finally, I will constantly be helping my sales team to improve their own self-image. Everything I have done and will do in the future will be designed to improve the self-image of each of our salespeople so that they have a better understanding of themselves as people of value who are doing a useful job in a way that makes clients glad to do business with them. Our overall team objective will be to seek satisfaction, because we know that the greatest unsatisfied need in the community today is the desire for satisfaction. And I will be the most surprised sales manager in the business if this team of mine isn't working at a rate of knots and selling space like you wouldn't believe.

Do my methods work? Yes, they do. How do I know they work? Because I have run a lot of different sales teams using these methods. Here is what happened to the first sales team I trained in the simple art of selling using the above methods.

My first experience in selling life assurance came when I joined the AMP as a salesperson. I set up my agency as a working agency and I wanted it to be very successful. The result was that in my first year I was awarded the Society's New South Wales branch award for the best new agent recruited that year. Three years later I was recruited into management as a unit sales manager in Sydney. I became the manager of Unit 24 at Parramatta which had only two salespeople and my objective was to build it into a winning team of first-class salespeople. Within three and a half years I had recruited and retained 26 agents and in that year my team was awarded the Society's New South Wales branch director's award for the most successful team that year (under the rules of the award). After becoming Sales Manager for Queensland, then for the New South Wales branch, I went to head office to become the Society's first marketing manager. Three years later I left to become a speaker on the international speaking circuit.

I wish you every success with your team and thank you for listening. Go in peace, be kind to yourselves and those you love and care for and thank you for having me at your conference.

3. The Hidden Buyer Motivators

I have been retained many times to deal with the problem of closing the sale, which is the final part of the sales process. Most successful salespeople are first-class networkers and they are great closers. They are not afraid to ask for the order. The not-so-successful salespeople worry about closing because they see the possibility of being seen to be pushy. Following are four powerful hidden motivators that will help you become a great closer. Asking for the order will not be difficult if you use these motivators. Every time you are near to closing a sale, remember: those who cannot ask cannot live. Let me begin my presentation.

Mr Chairman, thank you for your kind welcome and for inviting me to make this presentation on 'The Hidden Buyer Motivators'. Let me begin the way I start most of my presentations. Some people die at 30, but aren't buried till 70. Here lies the mind of an individual who at the age of 30 or more stopped thinking, was mentally dead and just waiting to be buried. I know this is not true of those who are here at this conference, but it is worth remembering that it can happen to anyone, at any time, unless they stay ahead of changes affecting us almost every day.

In this presentation I want to go over the critical issue of 'asking for the order' or as it is more commonly called, 'closing the sale'. It is critical in selling because we have to do much good work to get to the close and yet we often stumble at this last hurdle. Sometimes it is because we are not confident enough about asking for the order. Sometimes it is because we do not have a well-rehearsed sales presentation that has an effective way of asking for the order. To make your sales presentation more effective, I suggest you use the following hidden buyer motivators. They are powerful precisely because they are hidden.

Four powerful hidden buyer motivators

1. The obligation factor

The first of these built-in motivators is 'I help you and you help me' or the obligation factor. For centuries people have been setting up obligations by giving help to others which is returned when they want something. What you do to earn this reciprocity may be as simple as showing interest in what someone is doing. It may be as little as being seen at a function to honour or reward someone, or going to someone's wedding. The reason you received an invitation may have been as payback for a perceived action on your part; the invitation is seen as a payback by the person sending it. However you cause obligations to arise, there is always a desire — perhaps not even at a conscious level — to pay back by the person receiving something they perceive as favourable to them. This is a powerful influence and you should not underrate its importance to your sales success.

In the marketing and sales field the free gift, or 14-day free trial are all evidence that someone is either deliberately or accidentally exploiting the payback rule by creating an obligation within the mind of a prospect. So powerful is this obligation factor that most people will do everything they can to 'pay back' when the opportunity arises. Whenever you go the extra mile by way of a service or a gift you automatically embrace the power of the obligation factor. That's why salespeople who focus on improving the business or life of their prospects and customers are so successful. That's why networking creates influences that pay off in 'payback'. That's why building relationships is so productive. That's why paying constant attention to assisting your customers to succeed and prosper pays off in payback by them doing business with you.

2. Testimonials

Because most people are followers or imitators and only a very small percentage of the population are innovators it makes sense to add testimonials to your sales presentation. If the great majority are motivated more by what others do than by the proof of what you say about your product or service, then you should employ that motivator by using testimonials and endorsements showing how others are profiting by using your product or service. We see this motivator being used in all types of commercials when a well-known person endorses a product. We see it being used in selling books when a critic says 'buy this book' or when a book makes the best-seller list. We are influenced by critics to buy paintings, or attend restaurants that have just won an award, or to see a film because of rave reviews.

The proof that certain actors, products and services are socially acceptable is another powerful motivator. 'If others are doing it, then it's okay for me to follow' is how this motivator works. You can use this principle to get appointments. Your approach could be 'I would like to show you what other successful people in positions similar to yours are doing to increase their after-tax profits and spendable income. Are you interested in having more money to spend?' Do you have strong, powerful testimonials in your sales kit and do you use them? Are you using them in your advertising? If not, it's time to increase your sales success. If you want proof that testimonials work remember successful salespeople have been using them since selling was invented.

As Australia's best-selling business and self-help author I am constantly aware of those who endorse my books with testimonials saying how well a particular book of mine worked for them.

3. The friendship principle

Successful salespeople consistently use this buyer motivator to influence prospects to buy. It has always been the most successful prospecting method and is called referred lead prospecting. Yet despite its success it is the least used of all prospecting methods, probably because it entails asking for a direct favour. In using this method of buyer motivation in conjunction with the obligation principle the 'asking for a favour' problem disappears. Once you have established a 'payback' obligation no matter how small, the natural desire of the person you are asking to help with referrals is to do all they can to help you, because that fulfils their desire to pay back.

This payback obligation may arise because you have gone to a deal of trouble to make an outstanding presentation during which you have made offers to help solve your clients problem. If they have just purchased from you the obligation now exists. If you are given referrals you now have an obligation to them which you pay back by reporting back the results of your approach to their referral, saying thank you and showing appreciation of their help.

The referral method is effective because when you approach the prospect and use the name of your referrer you are giving an endorsement of you and your product or service that taps into the motivation of it being socially acceptable: 'My friend bought it so it must be okay for me'. It also embraces the results of many research projects which show that customers buy you first, then your idea to solve their problem, then your product or service to fund the idea and make it work. The friendship referral eliminates much of the need for you to sell yourself; the referral is doing that for you.

4. Seminar selling

This is an extremely powerful means of influencing people and tapping into hidden motivators, because most of the psychology of influence is present at the meeting. Fashion shows are just another name for this technique. Not enough retailers are using this method. It works because:

- A number of people are at the meeting, which confirms that it's okay to be there and it is a desirable topic to be considering.
- The presenter has credibility because of their position as an authority on the topic, so it's okay to take their suggested course of action.
- During the meeting testimonials are given by persons who attended a previous seminar, bought the offer and now say, 'This is how it has helped me', so it's okay for people to buy.
- When an individual sales approach is made to a prospect after the close of the seminar the payback principle is operating: *the seminar was free, it was good and it was put on for me and others. Now it's my turn to show my appreciation and payback.*

Nothing works all the time and with all people, but these hidden motivators are powerful and ever-present. They are not only used by us but are just as often used on us. They form a very powerful group of buyer motivations which lurk just below our consciousness, waiting for someone to trigger them off. We are largely powerless against them unless we have done a great deal of work in firstly recognising and understanding them and preparing techniques to combat them.

The principle of taking away

Here is a powerful technique that reinforces the hidden persuaders. It seems that people are more motivated when confronted with loss than they are towards making a gain.

It is very possible that much of the success we attribute to the benefits gained from the purchase of a product or service is more the result of the perceived loss a prospect will suffer if they don't buy. Do people buy shares because of the profits they make, or is the real motivator the lifestyle prestige and ego they will lose if they don't buy them, so that the profit is the way to avoid this loss? While this may sound like a play on words, current research indicates that the fear of loss is more powerful as a motivator than the prospect of a gain.

A key factor in some very successful advertising campaigns is scarcity. The promotion will run for three days after that you have lost out. The Three Tenors will be appearing for three performances and never again in this country. Once 200 of these plates are made the templates will be smashed and they will never be offered again. The return of The Beatles becomes a must-be-at event, because it is unlikely to happen again (in fact it will never happen again). Scarcity is another powerful buyer motivator, but everything that is sold is not scarce. The principle behind scarcity is that the perceived loss of whatever is now available can be generated by focusing on the loss of the value of the benefits if prospects don't buy. No matter how available the product or service, they have lost the benefits if they say no. The way to generate that feeling of loss is to generate a benefit and then focus on the loss incurred by not buying. Taking away is a powerful technique for creating buyer motivation and its use at the right time, combined with the hidden persuaders, can increase your selling performance dramatically.

Building a sales story

An effective sales presentation will encompass some of the above hidden motivators but to be truly effective they need to be contained in a sales story that as a presenter you know off by heart. Building it as you go is for amateurs. Professional salespeople have studied their prospects and clients and then built a sales story that can be told with confidence and great power, because they know what to say and when to say it. The way to build a winning presentation is by using it and noting what has power and is working and what is not working. Then take away what isn't working and build on what is working. Very soon you have a winning presentation and by including the hidden motivators you have increased your chances of success dramatically.

Selling by written presentations

Selling by written sales presentations is a most powerful way of gaining great success in your sales career. Written presentations take more time to prepare and they need a two-interview technique but their success ratio is very high. The first interview is to sell yourselves as a person of value, which encourages prospects to do business with you. Then it becomes a fact-finding interview; it is important that your prospect knows it is not a 'will you buy it now?' interview. Now your prospect can relax and you can get on with obtaining the information that will allow you to construct a solution to the problem and prepare it in a written sales track form. The major goal you have at this time is to sell yourselves as a person who has the ability to identify the problem and design a solution to the problem.

Now you can construct a winning written presentation containing your solution. Spend time preparing the written presentation. Enclose any necessary graphs and tables to make it easy for your prospect to understand what is needed to solve the problem. Have it in an attractive folder and have extra copies for others who may be taking part in the final interview. Have enough original copies for each person present. When they are reading it, stay silent unless you are asked a question, or they want clarification of some part of the presentation. Answer the question, or clarify the issue that led to the question. Do not keep talking, or start selling, or you will lose out. Silence is your friend and is working for you. When your prospect has finished reading your presentation, wait for them to talk. They know it is crunch time, decision time. If silence prevails just ask in a matter-of-fact voice, 'Can we proceed? Or is there any issue you need more clarification on?' You have now done all you can, so stay silent. Your prospect knows it's decision time and if you don't push you are more likely to win.

Written presentations are evidence that you are an innovator because others seeking your prospect's business will not go to the trouble of doing written presentations. You have at once separated yourselves from the crowd and given yourselves the chance not only to win the sale but to employ the friendship principle. You can be sure your prospect turned client will tell someone else about the salesperson who did such great work solving his problem. When it comes time to ask for referred leads you can be sure your client will be only too glad to show someone else how smart he was by referring you to them.

May you become a great innovator. Thank you for your interest in my presentation. It has been my pleasure to share this time with you. Go in peace and be kind to yourselves and those you love and care for. I wish you every success with your written presentations.

4. A Personal Leadership Challenge

Leadership is a constant item on the agenda of most discussions on how to manage and grow a business, irrespective of its size or its category. The key asset that leaders have to deal with is the human resource within the organisation. In order to deal best with the human resource, leaders must replace rank and power with mutual understanding and responsibility. One of the real issues that must be addressed by all leaders is that the old, tired and worn-out solutions of the past are no longer relevant today. Now it is 'innovate or die'. My comments should be seen as applying to top management and all those who are leaders of small groups within every level of management, whether they are in charge of five or fifty people. Let me begin my presentation.

Mr Chairman, thank you for your kind welcome to your conference and for your invitation to make this presentation.

There have been few times in our history when leadership has been needed more than now, because the challenges of our times are more pressing, more complex and more misunderstood in a general sense. Cries for leadership come from all sections of the community but no matter where they come from, or how they are expressed, they tell us one thing consistently: there is no one answer to all problems of an organisation just as there is no one way to lead, or to respond to the challenges of leadership. The challenge for one group of leaders is simply past history for another. The solutions for another group are the beginning of hope for others.

There is only one consistent thread in the search for leadership solutions and that is people. All the cries for leadership come from people and are answered by people. Leadership is a people problem and a personal leadership challenge is a personal people problem for each of those who aspire to be our leaders today. For some it will be a challenge that will be accepted for what it is: a real opportunity to grow as a person, for it is only under pressure that we respond and grow. It is the challenge that forces us out of our mental ruts to confront the issues of the future before they become the problems of today, nailing us to the present and inhibiting our ability to fulfil our potential.

If we just focus on leadership as one critical issue we are in danger of creating a narrow solution to a wider problem. Leadership in my view must embrace stewardship and responsibility if it is to drive us forward to a successful and happy future. We can be excellent managers but poor leaders. As Peter Drucker recently said, management is no longer a suitable name, in his opinion, because it implies a meaning which denotes authority and power, two out-of-date responses to the requirements of the current workplace. He went on to say that the traditional organisation of the last hundred years had an internal structure of rank and power. Today in a high-achieving organisation we must replace rank and power with mutual understanding and responsibility. When we do this we are getting to the core of true leadership qualities: vision, stewardship and responsibility.

Great leaders know that their only real resource is the intellectual capacity of the people who make up their organisation. They know that the qualities of a true leader encompass stewardship rather than control, and vision that offers direction and responsibility instead of demanding power. The challenges of the highly competitive, constantly and swiftly changing world in which we live and work demand not only a different approach to managing the enterprise, but a different response to the leadership challenge. Today, irrespective of the type of organisation we manage we must take more risks. We live in a high-risk world and as leaders we must take risks. With the taking of risks comes the probability of making mistakes, but I believe that the leaders of today and the future will owe as much to their mistakes as they will to their success, if they are to achieve their vision for the organisation they manage and lead.

Above all, we must accept that it is not the organisation but the people within it who are making the real contribution, not only to the organisation but to the community and our country. There is no such thing as a clever, far-sighted and innovative organisation. There are only organisations that are made up of clever, far-sighted and innovative individuals. A business has no life of its own. It is given life by the humans who work in it. No humans — no life and no business. Each of us as individuals make up the organisation in which we work. Money, buildings, machinery and other non-human assets don't think. Only humans solve problems, design winning products, write creative profit-building advertising, recruit, teach, motivate, inspire and develop other humans, solve problems and take advantage of opportunities. Everything other than the human resource in an organisation is only organised rubble and one day it will return to rubble.

We are living in a special time in history as the world comes to grips with change on a scale rarely, if ever, experienced before. As a result each of us as a leader needs to answer these questions:

- Am I being creative and innovative? Because today it is innovate or die.
- Am I encouraging the people in the organisation that I lead to become innovators?
- How can I find my way through the confusion and chaos of all this change?
- What will the changes mean to me and the organisation I lead?
- What must I do to be an effective and productive part of this new society?
- What strategy should I implement to ensure that I make the most of the opportunities and drive the organisation I lead into a more productive and rewarding future?

While the task is daunting, the challenge is exciting and full of the promise of a future more rewarding than we can at this time imagine. It is part of mankind's evolutionary process to face, conquer and move on. We have always been at our best during times of great change and challenges and this time will be no exception. The majority will grow and prosper as a result of solving today's problems. A minority will fail the test and be found wanting and as a result they will become the casualties of today's changes.

That some win and some lose has always been our history. The message for each of us is to be among those who win and move on to fresh challenges. We can make certain of that result by being prepared and innovative. The first step in preparation is to identify as best we can the broad trends that are shaping the change and then clarify the specific issues we must confront. All challenges must be seen and acted upon as new opportunities. We need to develop a can-do and will-do attitude and respond as if everything is possible. Remember, if you do not embrace these changes then you will become a casualty of them. If you embrace them and help develop them, you will most certainly benefit from them. Think *capacity* and *innovation* and build a new and different you. Focus on your own intellectual capacity and stretch it to reach your true potential. The block to achieving our potential is that we see ourselves tomorrow as we are today, forever. It is time to change today so that your tomorrows can be more exciting, enjoyable and rewarding. Who knows what you are truly capable of?

The impact on each of us as individuals is that we need to focus on improving our personal intellectual capacity. The constant need for each of us will be to keep up; school is never out for the knowledge worker. Those who accept the challenge will survive and prosper while those who procrastinate and try to get by on yesterday's skills and knowledge will slowly sift to the bottom of the heap. As a consequence they will become the casualties of the changes they either would not, or could not make.

The outcome of this awareness of intellectual capacity must be to turn what we know into effective results. Business is already progressing in the shift from process to results and we can expect to hear a great deal more about outcomes and results and innovation as a basic requirement of every facet of our enterprise. This shift to results and innovation is part of the change that is taking place in business organisational structures today. In your particular occupation it will be no different. It's change or perish — and therein lies the problem, for humans resist change. We can observe in the daily news the number of organisations that are having problems because they are living in the past instead of the future, many always have and the reason they do so is their adherence to their past work practices and mind-sets, their paradigms. Your success as a leader will be determined by how well you manage your occupational paradigm. All humans are restricted by their particular paradigms. We filter incoming data through our paradigms and as a result we see very clearly what we usually see and expect to see, but when the data is new and unexpected we often either ignore it, or fail to see it. Remember, we tend to see what we want to see, we hear what we want to hear, and believe to be true what we want to be true. As a result most of us expect tomorrow to be like today forever and we continue to try to solve today's problems with yesterday's solutions. In effect we seek the future by looking through yesterday's eyes.

Understanding paradigms is critical to your future for a very important reason, which is that change with all its ramifications is going to be coming at you at an ever-increasing rate forever. Unless you can see it with new eyes you may miss your chance. The following example is a classic illustration of a paradigm. The owner of an upmarket manufacturing business came to one of my seminars. Afterwards he rang and asked me if I would come and see him at his business. I arrived and he showed me around his workshop and showrooms. His product was top of the range. He said his problem was that some retailers were importing similar products from Asia which came in by ship in pallets and were undercutting him in price by at least fifty per cent. They were literally putting him out of business. He asked me whether I could show him how to deal with this problem. I asked 'How many pallets do you bring in?'

He said 'I don't bring in stock. I make it.'

I replied with 'You are an expert. Your competitors can't compete with you in terms of expertise so why don't you compete on expertise. You will win hands down.' I left him with that suggestion. He didn't take my advice because his upmarket manufacturing of a high quality product paradigm stopped him from achieving outstanding success. Within two years he went out of business.

Remember, you see life through your particular paradigm so the issue is to work smarter, not harder, and search for the new directions that your organisation should take in terms of its products, services, advertising and so on. The blocks to achieving our true leadership potential are precisely the same as those that inhibit all organisations. We see ourselves as we are today and project our future based on who we are, rather than on who and what we could become. We do the same with the organisations we manage. Just as organisations and countries have to reinvent themselves, so we need to reinvent

ourselves. We can best do that by *what-ifing*. By asking
ourselves:

- What can I do to dramatically increase my personal
  potential as a leader?
- What is my strategy for me as a leader?
- Do I have a marketing plan for me as a leader?
- On a scale of 1 to 7, how do I rate as a leader?
- Am I matching my potential to the key issues I see
  emerging in the marketplace today?
- Am I reinventing myself as a leader?
- Am I encouraging stewardship, vision and responsibility
  and discarding rank and power?
- Am I being an innovator and asking the people in the
  organisation that I lead to follow my example?

Let's look at some present trends and reflect on whether
they really cause us to realise our true potential. Ask
yourselves these questions:

- Does my present way of doing things really inspire
  and focus me and my team on the real potential of
  our organisation?
- Or does it focus me on my own, or someone else's
  past achievements?
- Does the methodology of my systems bury me in
  detail and inhibit me and my team from using our
  real abilities to reach our true potential?
- Or does it fire the imagination, stir creativity and
  encourage innovation?

For imagination, creativity and innovation are the stuff of reaching our true potential as an effective leader.

The good news: will it all be easy? For some it will and for others it won't. Will it be impossible? For a very few it will, but for most it won't. Remember, this is the age of the individual. It is the greatest time in the history of mankind for the individual to flourish and prosper. It is time for each of us to assert our right to the future we long to have, but if we accept it is the age of the individual we must also accept that the responsibility to make it happen in our life belongs to the individual — to you and me.

Here is more good news. As a human being you have the power of choice in your life. You can choose between options. Of all known life in the universe, we are the only species that can choose. So choose wisely. Choose success not failure, choose happiness not sadness, choose mutual understanding and responsibility instead of rank and power; choose to be a leader who will not only have a new and exciting vision of the future but the courage and determination to bring it to reality and to reward those who have assisted you in achieving those outcomes.

Becoming a great leader means creating a stewardship culture. That means overcoming deeply ingrained and consolidated beliefs, attitudes and practices that are present in some degree in people at all levels of an organisation, including yourselves. We are the product of a patriarchal society; many of us either want to be a good parent at work, or we want to work with and for a good parent. When we move to stewardship instead of management and create ways for individuals to govern themselves, we find that many of them don't want a partnership, they want a parent, or they want to become a parent. Some don't want to give up the power and rank of the parent. The only way to empower an organisation is by stewardship so that each individual contributes to and becomes responsible for the organisation.

Great leaders have vision. They become their own futurists, they are forever looking up and forward. They have a great capacity to dream and an unrelenting determination to make their vision and dream a reality. When a leader consistently, enthusiastically and clearly articulates their vision the response from those included in that vision is dramatic. Once the vision is strong enough and clear enough to touch people personally then it becomes enshrined in each individual's goals and again the results are dramatic. Leadership is won, not bestowed. Titles are given. Leadership is unselfish, glory is shared. Great leaders get intense satisfaction firstly by knowing they are performing to their potential, but equally by knowing they are growing their people. They know their real test is how well they have developed the human resource in their organisation. True leaders know that mutual trust is the glue that binds an organisation's people together and develops a climate in which each person not only feels free to perform to their potential but feels responsible to do so.

Outstanding leaders are creative in their outlook; they consistently encourage everyone in the organisation to look for the creative alternative and go for it. They are courageous in decision-making and they have the inner strength and commitment to keep going when it would be easier and more comfortable to give up on an issue. Perhaps the quality most admired by those who follow great leaders is the humility of their leader. They are little different when enjoying a victory as when enduring a loss. They share the success and make little of failures. Leaders thrive on change and, as I recall Douglas Long once said, leaders recognise that whatever is being done today is being done in the most up-to-date, obsolete way possible. So recognise that what you are now doing is on the way to obsolescence and will remain so until you find a better way to do it. Today it is innovate or die.

The search for new and better solutions that will grow and develop the organisation and the people you lead must be your number one priority if you are to be a true leader. In your endeavours to reach this goal do not let yourselves be deterred by those with less vision, a weaker commitment and a stronger desire to live in the present until it becomes the past. When you are told, 'Don't do it that way, it would be much easier to do it this way', remember that, as Neil Simon said, if Michelangelo had taken that advice he would have painted the Sistine floor and his masterpiece would soon have been lost forever beneath the trudging feet of the people who look down in search of certainty and safety instead of up to the challenges of the future — which is the true goal of all effective leaders.

Thank you for listening and may great success come your way.

5. You'll Earn a Fortune

I have given this presentation hundreds of times, and because the audience interest is exceptionally high, I find the presentation usually takes at least three hours. Afterwards the questions come for as long as I can stay and answer them. Building wealth in our lives is an issue for all of us, irrespective of the income we earn. Remember, you will earn a fortune if your working life is over a normal duration. Time does not stand still and the sooner we start building wealth in our lives the sooner we can become financially independent. As you read this chapter, focus on what you need to do to create wealth in your life and then do it. The sooner you begin, the easier it is to become financially independent. Let me begin.

Mr Chairman, thank you for your kind welcome to your conference and for your invitation to make this presentation. Let me remind you that school is never over for those who want to survive and prosper in this new and different marketplace. There is no future in the past. The title of my presentation is 'You'll Earn A Fortune'. In my opinion you will never get a better opportunity to ensure your financial future than by following the advice given in this presentation. Let me begin.

From your first to your last pay cheque you will earn a fortune if you have a working life of normal duration. You may be self-employed, or work for an enterprise — every time you carry out your normal working activity you are earning part of that fortune. In fact, creating wealth is what you are currently doing. *You are a money machine.* Whether you have a definite plan to increase and keep much of that wealth is a different, but critical issue if you want to become financially independent.

'You'll Earn a Fortune' is about becoming life-focused, setting financial goals, developing a plan of action to achieve those goals and above all sticking to the plan until you have achieved them and become financially independent. It is about taking charge of your life and not becoming dependent on chance for your success. Always remember, every day of your life you are earning part of your fortune and you must, if you are genuine about achieving financial independence, set aside from everyday living expenses part of what you earn and put it to work in your financial plan. No one else will do it for you. It is your dream; now it is time to make it come true.

Why is this important to you and why should you start now if you have not already established a plan to create financial independence in your life? Because every day counts. There is not a minute to lose if you want to finish a winner in the race to financial independence. Here is a statistical summary of our financial chances in life.

The march through life of 100 people aged 25
By the time they reach the age of 65
Approximately 24 will be dead.
54 will be living on assisted incomes.
16 will still be working.
5 will retire on a livable income.
1 will be wealthy.

If you had a choice, where would you like to be?

These statistics, originally from the US 20 years ago, should be used as guidelines only. Statistics change over time as they reflect the changes taking place in our every-day lives. Massive changes in the working environment have taken place. Health care has improved greatly. But human behavioural traits do not change dramatically, so we go on doing what we go on doing. No doubt some changes in the above statistics have taken place, but with few exceptions they will not be massive. They tell us how the good intentions of so many of us simply languish in the shadows of our life, not because of the lack of opportunity to make them come true, but because of the lack of action to put them into practice.

Where will you finish if you continue your current course? Where would you like to finish? Do you want to be one of the five out of 100 who have become financially independent? Would you prefer to be the one in 100 who on average finishes wealthy? I imagine you would like to avoid being among the 54 who do not become financially independent. You can be certain of one thing, you will become part of these statistics, for they are the story of our lifetime. You can also be certain that it is rarely too late to influence your outcome. By living a healthy lifestyle you can even improve your chances of not joining the first group. If you adopt and work a healthy financial plan you can be certain you won't join the other groups who for whatever reason didn't make it to financial independence.

Start now to work your plan. Will it be difficult? Perhaps for some it will, but for none will it be impossible. These statistics are the story of human life in financial terms and they portray in stark reality what the outcome is, despite the fact that most of us think, 'It won't happen to me'. You, like me, know that if we were talking to 100 young people aged 25 about their chances in life and we asked them what their financial situation would be when they retired at 65, most would tell us that they would be retired at 50, travelling the world and spending their fortune. Yet the statistics tell us the real story.

Most of us who enjoy constant employment and a long working life will earn a fortune. To convince yourselves that this is true you only have to apply the following example to your own life. You will find that, given good health and employment either in your own or someone else's business, you will earn a fortune in your working life. Use as an example a person 20 years of age who has recently started work. Take into account their normal earnings based over their working lifetime of say 40 years. Add in the wage rises they can expect, plus an allowance for inflation and you will find that they will earn during their working life of 40 years something in the order of $3 million to $5 million.

This exercise does not take into account the fact that many people will earn a great deal more than this example simply because they will have not only received normal wage rises, but they will have increased their personal effectiveness to the extent that they could easily double, or treble their earning capacity. But earning extra is no guarantee of accumulating wealth, because many increase their standard of living each time their earning capacity increases, which eats up the extra income. Their standard of living improves but their savings and investments don't grow. If you delay improvements to lifestyle and invest the money it won't be long before you can have the money and the lifestyle.

Most of us think of investing as putting money into either shares or property. We think of wealth as being the result of those kinds of investments and too often we assume we do not have the money to get involved in investing. But why do so few of us ignore one of the best ways of creating wealth in our lives? A way that needs very little money. A way that almost all of us can follow. *It's called self-improvement. The best way to get more dollars in your life is to earn them. Why not improve your abilities in whatever field you choose so that you will earn an extra $10,000 or $20,000 or $50,000 or more in your annual wage or salary?*

Think it through; you must know a lot of people who have done just that. You may even have done it yourselves. If you have, congratulations. Think: if you improve yourselves to the extent you can earn another $10,000 a year after tax, you will receive a salary dividend in your pay equal to someone else investing $100,000 a year at 10 per cent compound interest. You will be in the same situation after only having to invest some time and effort into self-development. If you get to an increase of $50,000 a year it is the same as someone with money investing $500,000 a year at 10 per cent compound interest. Not long ago your chances of improving yourselves quickly and being rewarded quickly were not good. Doing that would have meant being employed over a lifetime in one career position. Now it is different; there are no lifelong careers with one organisation. You can develop yourselves in many different ways and as soon as you get more ability someone will pay you for it. Moving into different positions is now the normal way to go and you can do it. Why do I say this is one of the best ways to create wealth in your life? Because I have done it and I know you can do it.

Even if you continue to work in a position that will receive normal pay rises for inflation and so on, you will earn a fortune. Imagine how big that fortune could be if you focused on self-improvement. Every time you increase your ability and knowledge you increase your potential, which means you can get paid more. You don't have to wait around. You can go out and market yourselves. What a wonderful opportunity.

Here is just one true story, taken from personal experience, that illustrates my point about the fortune we earn. I was travelling by plane from Sydney to Adelaide to speak at a national conference. After takeoff and when we had settled into the flight, the man sitting next to me started a conversation and we exchanged names and occupations, as business people do. He was the CEO of a large company and appeared to be in his late sixties. I was a former AMP marketing manager, now a speaker on the international speaking circuit. Our general conversation was about what was happening in the economy, and he made the comment, 'It's hard to make a dollar these days', to which I responded, 'I don't think it is hard to make a dollar.' He said, 'Jack, you must move in different circles to me.' I responded with the 'You'll Earn a Fortune' story I am relating in this chapter, saying, 'It's not hard to earn a dollar, it's only hard to save it.' To which he agreed.

I then asked him, 'Would you like to do these sums in your head? Don't tell me the numbers, just do the maths. From your first to your present pay cheques, calculate how much you have earned and tell me, do you think you have earned a fortune?'

There was silence while he did the maths and then he said, 'Jack, you're right. I have earned a fortune — millions — and sadly, I haven't saved as much as I should have.'

I went on to discuss the principle of paying yourself first and we had a long conversation on the reasons why we don't always do it. He was most interested in the 'You'll Earn a Fortune' story and asked many questions.

Our journey ended and we went our separate ways. But just as I was leaving the luggage area someone tapped me on the shoulder. When I looked around it was my fellow traveller. He said, 'Jack, I want to thank you for your views on earning and saving from the fortune we earn. It's a pity I didn't meet you sooner, because I would have been a lot richer than I am now if I had. Thank you again. I never thought of life and earning like that.' I guess he, like most, was too busy earning a fortune to be concerned with keeping a fortune.

You can be certain that, given a normal work experience, you will at the end of your working lifetime have earned a fortune. The critical question is: how much of it will you have left when you finish your working life? Remember, when you have finished work all that is left to look forward to is whatever your accumulated savings can earn for you, because there are only three ways of creating wealth — a man at work, a woman at work, or a dollar. When your normal working life is finished and retirement beckons, if you have not saved enough dollars to put to work to take the place of your normal working earnings then you basically have three options:

1. Go on working to earn the dollars you need to keep enjoying your current lifestyle.

2. Lower your lifestyle to fit your decrease in earnings.
3. Live either totally, or partially on someone else's money by getting a government pension. (Let me say now that there is nothing wrong with getting a pension. The truth is, you have earned it by way of the taxes you have paid over your working life.)

Let's do another illustration, this time taking a person aged 35 who is currently earning $60,000 a year. If that person keeps on earning the same amount for the next 25 years plus all increases in salary and a reasonable rate of inflation, that person will also earn in the vicinity of $3 million to $5 million. As always, the critical question is: how much will that person have left to put to work when he or she can no longer earn income? It is important to ask the same question of women as of men because many women will be the major breadwinner at the conclusion of their working life. As more and more marriages break down and more women elect to not marry, this issue is of critical importance to them. Fortunately, many women are now very successful in their own businesses, or have become high-earning career professionals. But the problem of saving enough from earned income which is then invested to deliver the dollars needed to earn income in retirement is still a real issue in the lives of many individuals. Despite the reality that the great majority of us will earn a fortune during our working lives there are too many of us who do not seem to understand or appreciate this simple concept. If you want to overcome the problem of not enough dollars in your retirement, you need to take action now. Use another concept that will solve your problem: pay yourself first.

There are only three ways to create wealth

Leaving aside gifts, or what you might inherit, there are only three ways to create wealth. The first way is a man at work, the second is a woman at work and the third is money at work. In our case the money is the Australian dollar. Time equals money. How often have we heard that statement? Yet the reality of life for the great majority of us is that work equals money. If you think time equals money, stop work and see how much money you make unless you have dollars at work. A man or a woman at work, or a dollar at work, are the realities of making money and creating wealth. If you are not working and have no dollars at work you can be sure you won't be making money.

The wealth we accumulate through our working life starts with the income we earn; that is, a man or a woman at work. If we can save and set aside some of that income on a regular basis then we have dollars that we can put to work in the share or property market, or we can become self-employed and have our own business which could be involved in one or more types of enterprise. Our chances of accumulating wealth increase dramatically by putting dollars to work as well as enjoying the returns from our own labour. If you win wealth you win it as a result of the price that you invest to buy the ticket. Even when you inherit wealth it is probably the result of a lot of time and effort for which you originally did not get paid before you ultimately received your reward in terms of an inheritance. In many cases gifts are received as the result of extended effort one way or another on the part of the person receiving the gift. As a result of that effort, someone is willing to make a gift because they see whatever has been done as being worthy of their gift.

In reality a man or a woman at work, or a dollar at work, is the truth of our financial life and in many ways we can put that truth to work as a concept in our life to achieve financial independence. We may be selling any one of a thousand different products or services. We may follow any one of a hundred different occupations, we may invest our money in many different ways and yet the reality still remains: no man or woman at work and no dollar at work usually means no wealth and very little hope of financial independence.

It is a common human trait to delude ourselves into thinking that wealth somehow or other will magically appear in our life. The thought of becoming instantly wealthy occupies most minds at some stage. But if there is not a workable plan in action based on the realities of life rather than unrealistic expectations, then our chances of achieving wealth become just that — a chance that somehow at some time good fortune will bring us wealth. By all means buy your lottery ticket and at least have a chance of winning instant wealth, but remember it is the investment in the ticket that makes it possible to win. It's just a dollar at work. There are many different ways of taking a gamble to win something rather than working over a longer term to get it. It is a fact that whilst the possibility of winning is always present, the odds are that more will lose than win because if they don't the winners can't get paid. Because it is the losers who pay the winners. It is also a fact that some of those who win instant wealth soon lose it very quickly for they have never before had the opportunity to learn how to deal with wealth. Those who accumulate wealth over longer periods have learned how to live with it because it did not all come at once. Many of those who have won wealth have gone public to say how difficult it was to adapt to unexpected wealth and that they were happier before they won it. These comments are not made to inhibit your outlook on winning wealth, they are made so you will keep winning in perspective and see that earning great wealth is more satisfying than winning it. Earning success through our own efforts is what makes life exciting and interesting, because we did it. We made the plan and *we did it*!

Accomplishment is the basis of motivation. Often I have been told by very successful individuals that the journey was the exciting and fulfilling part of their life. The monetary success was the scoreboard. For these people, setting the goal and making the plan and then working the plan to achieve great success was the part that gave them the most pleasure.

Pay yourself first

One of life's great problems is that most people earn their income, pay their way, spend money on what they need and like and try to save something of what is left. In most cases there is none, or too little left so the fortune they earn simply gets spent. Over 30 years ago, I came across this inspiring thought: *If on the other hand each of us were to adopt the practice of paying ourselves first and spending what was left, most of us would revolutionise our chances of becoming financially independent.* If in paying ourself first we were to pay 15 per cent to 20 per cent from each and every pay cheque of our earnings and place it in an investment that earned a reasonable return, we would very swiftly accumulate a sizeable amount of capital. As soon as we were able to, we could then make a down-payment on real estate, the first purchase of which should be our own home. The money we save on paying rent can pay off our home mortgage and we could continue to invest in the share or property market. In no time at all the concepts of 'You'll earn a fortune' and 'Paying yourself first' will be working in your life to create a secure and profitable financial future. If these concepts do nothing more than focus your thinking on your life and the challenge and opportunity to become financially independent, they will have proven to be of great value to you.

If you use the concepts of 'You'll earn a fortune' and 'Paying yourself first' to create wealth in your life you will not only have absorbed two of life's great lessons, you will have overcome the major reasons why so many never attain financial independence. Unfortunately our education system does not teach the simple concepts that are so valuable and important to each of us. It is also a sad but true fact that many parents did not learn the lesson themselves and therefore cannot pass it on to their own children. If you want to win in life and become financially independent then you need to employ these concepts now. You can then be certain that when you finish work you will have the dollars to keep earning for you. In deciding how much you should set aside and what the returns would be over a set period of time you need a further concept: the magic of 72.

The magic of 72

Number 72 is a key figure in assisting you to do calculations in your head or easily on paper when dealing with earnings, rates of return, the duration of an investment, and so on. For example, if you make an investment with an interest rate of 8 per cent and you want to know how long you will have to leave the money invested before your initial investment is doubled, you divide the interest rate of 8 per cent into 72. It goes nine times, which means that if you invest $1000 at 8 per cent, in nine years it will have doubled to $2000. In a further nine years the $2000 will have doubled to $4000. In a period of 18 years commencing from the date of the first investment of your $1000 you will have accumulated $4000 without having invested any other money, provided the interest rate maintained is 8 per cent. It is possible therefore to calculate on into the future, doubling the total every nine years. If on the other hand you want to double your money every four years, you divide four into 72 and that gives you the interest rate you need to earn to double your money in four years; in this case it's 18 per cent. You can either calculate returns and growth rates by the interest rate divided into 72 which gives you the duration over which the investment has to take place to double your investment, or you can select a period of time in which you want your investment to double, such as 12 years, and divide that into 72, which gives an interest rate of 6 per cent to achieve that goal.

Let's do some calculations on the term needed to double our investment at a given rate of interest by dividing the interest rate into 72:

- 6 per cent equals 12 years
- 10 per cent equals 7.2 years
- 15 per cent equals 4.8 years (This has been the return on shares over the last decade.)
- 24 per cent equals 3 years

Now let's do some calculations based on a given term by dividing the term into 72:

- 6 years equals 12 per cent
- 8 years equals 9 per cent
- 10 years equals 7.2 per cent
- 15 years equals 4.8 per cent

This method of quick calculation can be used by people who sell real estate or investment products, making it easy for them to calculate very quickly the growth rate in compound interest terms that an investment must achieve to double its value over any given period. Or you can establish the growth in any investment over the past X number of years and apply that growth rate to give you the number of years it will take to double the value of the investment.

You could as well do the calculations on any commodity using the current rate of inflation. Divide the current rate of inflation into 72 and that is the period over which you will need to double your investments to maintain a rate equal to inflation. You can apply the principle to mortgages, buying or selling any commodity, or in any number of ways to illustrate values in terms of earnings and growth rate. Being able to do these calculations in your head will certainly make it easier for you to assess the value of any investment you are considering.

A note of caution! Often the sale figures for a property are reported in the news as 'Fred Investor purchased this property six years ago for X dollars and has sold it for X plus dollars' and the reader is left with the conclusion that if you subtract the purchase price from the sale price this is your profit. It looks great; however, if you were able to factor in the legal fees involved in the process of buying and selling, the cost of stamp duty, the amount of borrowing costs, the property maintenance costs, the rates, the insurance, the selling costs of advertising, agent's commission and, on some properties, land tax, then get a net profit figure and divide that by six to cover the six years Fred owned the property, you would have the real rate of return excluding inflation.

Whatever you do and whatever the investment, be sure you always get the *net* profit and then divide it by the term or duration of the investment. Assuming unreal rates of return on any investment can cost you heaps and lead you to make unsound investments. For example, we may read that Fred Investor bought this house six years ago for $350,000 and has just sold it for $700,000. What an investment! Doubled his buying price in only six years! If we divide 72 by the six years we find that the house value grew by only 12 per cent compound interest. Not too much magic in that. Of course, Fred investor probably did much better than that because he may have bought the house with mostly borrowed money. The leveraging effect of borrowed money could have made the investment pay off at a much better than 12 per cent compound interest rate. On the other hand, the purchasing and selling costs plus interest on borrowings, maintenance and so on have not been taken into account. All of which says, be sure you calculate profit on real costs so that you know how much you actually made.

Here is an example based on my own home. If the purchase price is subtracted from the selling price the return on investment is very high. If we take account of what I have spent on maintenance such as repainting both inside and outside, developing gardens, building on a studio for my artwork, developing patios, paying rates, insurance, interest on the original loan, buying costs, selling costs and so on, I would have probably done a lot better in the share market because statistics show that over any 20-year term in the past 100 years shares earned a higher return than property. The advantage you have with buying your home is that you have to keep investing by way of forced saving and that plus leveraging is what makes a home a good investment. It is also tax free, which is another great reason to invest in your own home before you buy investment property.

It is accepted that both the property and share market have gone through boom times and bust times, and there have always been the exceptions to any given rule — even in tough times some investors, regardless, made great returns. It is equally true that in good times there have been some investors who have made losses. In making money there are no sure-fire, never-lose investments. The quicker the time in which you want to achieve financial independence, the greater the risk. The longer the term you set yourselves, the easier it is to achieve financial independence. Getting rich slowly is not difficult. As pioneering IBM president, Thomas J. Watson said:

All the problems of the world could be settled easily if men were only willing to think. The trouble is that men very often resort to all sorts of devices in order not to think, because thinking is such hard work.

Most of us would agree with him because it is hard work, but it does pay off, especially in self-development.

How soon are you willing to get started if you have not already done so? If you are already investing, check what you are doing against the above concepts and decide if you should change some of what you are doing to build on the fortune you will earn. While you are doing this, you should test your actions and goals against another concept.

Live, die or quit

The 'live, die or quit' rule is one of the most powerful concepts we can use because it is real and it applies to every one of us in every aspect of our life. For example, if your current plan is to build a new home then you will either live to see the home completed, or you will die before the home is completed, or you will quit building the home for reasons as yet unforeseen and you will do something else. If your aim and ambition is to earn $100,000 a year in your work you will either live to accomplish your plan, or you will die before you do, or you will quit for reasons unforeseen now and set yourselves different goals. If your ambition is to retire before you're 50 you will live to accomplish your ambition or you will die before you do, or you will quit and change your plans for reasons unforeseen now. If you want to travel the world you will live to travel the world, die before you do, or you will quit and change your plans for reasons unforeseen now. If you want to be self-employed and go into business on your own account, you will live to have your own business, or you will die before you do, or you'll quit that goal for reasons unforeseen now and do something else.

Live, die or quit is a reality in life for each and every one of us. You can use it to focus on the three choices each of us has whenever we set our mind to achieving a goal. Achieving financial independence is no exception when it comes to live, die or quit. You will either live to become financially independent, or you will die before you do, or you will quit for reasons unforeseen now and settle for whatever comes your way.

As live, die or quit is a reality for every one of us, your decisions in relation to becoming financially independent should be based on those three issues. What will happen if you live? What would be the implications of this action on your family if you die and what are the options and the possible outcomes if you quit? Understanding the reality of these issues and how they affect your plans and goals is critical to your success in achieving financial independence. The real reason why most people do not achieve financial independence in their life is that they do not focus enough on what they want to achieve and they don't seem to understand that, like every other human, any of their ventures are subject to the three possible outcomes of live, die or quit. Taking them into consideration when you are making your plans will enable you to set your goals to achieve the best possible outcomes from your efforts. Make no mistake, this concept is working in your life every day — now and forever.

Developing ourselves

One of the greatest wealth development plans you can put into place is to develop yourself until you are earning a very high income each and every year. This gives you a wonderful opportunity to invest more easily. If you increase your income with the goal of putting much of that income into a profitable investment or investments, you are increasing your chances greatly of becoming wealthy. If you do this you will be a winner. For most people, each time they earn more they increase their standard of living accordingly and thus give away the opportunity of building wealth in their life and simply live for the day. If you can avoid this problem you will become a winner.

What holds us back from going after the goal of financial independence? Is it that we feel we have plenty of time and therefore do not start now, and the dream just fades away as we spend now and plan to save and invest later? Is it because we fear failure and do nothing, which generally guarantees the failure we fear? Is it procrastination and we can't get started? Is it that we live for the moment because it seems to be more important than the future? Is it that we are just not interested? Or is it because our vision of ourselves isn't big enough, or that we are not confident in our own ability? Are outside events holding us back? Whatever the reason that delays or stops us from achieving our goal of reaching financial independence, we owe it to ourselves and those we love and care for to rethink the issue. We need to start now to build wealth in our lives. Start by paying yourself first and taking what you pay yourself and build it into the fortune you can have if you only get going — and now is the best time. Every day counts.

As you do your planning on how to develop wealth in your life, go to the chapter on 'Goal-achieving' and make your plans and set your goals according to the method shown in that presentation. I have used that method in my working career and afterwards in my new career as a speaker/presenter. It is the best goal-achieving method I have ever seen. It will work miracles for you if you use it exactly as it is described. Whatever you do, don't become a 'some day' or 'maybe tomorrow' person, for it may cost you your chance to build wealth in your life. Go to it now: it can be the most exciting time of your life.

Thank you for listening. I have enjoyed every minute of my time with you today. Go in peace. Be kind to yourselves and those you love and care for, and remember, opportunity is knocking. Embrace it, now!

6. Dealing with the Unexpected

Audience response to a presentation is always about how they see it applying to themselves. If there is no response then the presentation has not been very successful. The only life in a business is the humans who make up the human resource of the business. We may be talking business techniques but the business has no understanding of such techniques. It is the human resource that gives the business life — a reason to exist; no humans, no business. I am always concerned about the human response to what I have to say because unless what I have said has some perceived value to my audience then my presentation was not successful. Happily I can say that I have had wonderful responses to my presentations. Sometimes there have been unexpected responses by some of the individuals who were attending them. Some of those responses are mentioned in this chapter.

Kwik Kopy Conference

I have good memories of being the keynote speaker for the annual Kwik Kopy conference that was held in Leura in the

Blue Mountains, west of Sydney. I had been retained to give them a presentation based on my best-selling book, *Yes You Can*, which has three segments: Mind, Time and Goals. When it was time to make my presentation I walked to the lectern and as I did so I noticed a table with two chairs over to the right of where I was speaking. It was unusual to position seating in front of the audience and to the side of the speaker. Whoever sat there would not be infringing on my space, but I wondered why the table and chairs were there.

As I began the presentation, two men walked in from the back of the audience and sat at the table. The older of the two produced a pen and paper and started taking notes as I spoke. My attention was on the audience because they were the reason I was there. From time to time I noticed that the man with the notepaper continued to write and I wondered whether that was good or bad.

The presentation took approximately three hours with a break in between each of the three sessions. The breaks were short so I only had time to focus on preparing for the next session. The response from the audience was very positive and at the end of the presentation I answered many questions from the audience. When the question sessions ended I received a standing ovation.

After I had collected the slides and notes I had used for the presentation, the man who had been taking notes came over and said, 'Son, that is the best presentation I have heard in years. Usually when I like a session I take four or five pages of notes. I want to pay you the compliment of letting you know that I have taken 16 pages of notes. I believe you and I have something in common so I would be pleased if you would have dinner with me tonight so we can continue our conversation.' We agreed on a time and place and he left.

Later, I spoke with the franchise owner who had hired me to do the presentation and told him of this meeting. When I asked who the two men were, he told me the man who had invited me to dinner was the worldwide owner of the Kwik Kopy franchise and the man with him had the Kwik Kopy franchise for Canada.

That evening I had dinner with Bud, who told me how he had come to be the owner of the Kwik Kopy franchise worldwide. It was a wonderful story: he had set up a small one-man printing business and when the new copy machines started to impact on his business he developed the Kwik Kopy concept, organising the structure and franchising the business worldwide.

Bud then told me that the reason he wanted to meet and talk with me was that he understood from my presentation that he and I were travelling the same spiritual road. He told me that he belonged to a group of very successful American businessmen who had for some years met on a regular basis to share their successes and experiences. He said that each member of the group had a number of copies of a special book they used to chart their course for success and when they met someone they believed was ready to use this book in their life they gave them a copy.

Bud then said, 'Jack, I'm only here for a day and half and I did not expect to meet anyone who in my view was ready for this book, so I didn't bring any spare copies with me, but I do have my own book and I would like to give it to you. It's marked with highlight and other notes I have made but perhaps these may even help you as they have me.' He then gave me his copy of the book *Dynamic Thought*. I have treasured this book, firstly because it was given to me by Bud, an outstanding human being, and secondly because the book has been of great value to me. I have read it many times until it has become for me what it was to Bud. It is on my desk at my right hand and I read it in part on a regular basis. It reflects much of what I have written in my best-selling book *Yes You Can*.

At the conclusion of our dinner Bud said he would like me to come to America and make my presentation of 'Yes You Can' to his annual franchisee conference. My visit had to be put on hold and I never made the trip. However, the memory of that wonderful man and his gift to me will stay with me forever. Only last month I rang and made contact with him again and let him know how valuable his gift has been to me. We had a long conversation about life in general and his current situation specifically. He is a great human being. Warm and friendly and concerned about the welfare of others.

Rotorua – a technical hitch

On one of my visits to New Zealand a promoter retained me to go to Rotorua to do a night-time seminar based on my book *Yes You Can*. I had been to Rotorua several times before and was looking forward to being there again.

At 7.30 pm the promoter introduced me and I started the presentation, which was scheduled to go for three hours including two ten-minute breaks. All my presentations were on slides and at that time I spoke only from the slides which I used to prompt me; I did not have any written notes.

Fifteen minutes into the presentation, the slide projector ceased to operate. A swift inquiry told me there was no other projector available in Rotorua so for the next two hours and 45 minutes I spoke from memory. I was fortunate that I was making a presentation that I had given over a hundred times and so the memory test was not all that difficult. At the end of the presentation the audience gave me a standing ovation. To this day I'm not sure whether it was because of the quality of my presentation or because they believed I had handled so well the problem of no notes and no slides.

From that night onwards, I have always spoken word for word from prepared notes and used slides to keep the audience interested. Fortunately, the problem has never happened again. It did, however, reinforce to me that preparation is a key issue, no matter what we are tackling in life. We should always be asking, 'What if this happened? What if that happened? How would I handle it?' So the lesson was a good one, and one that I think is worth passing on: remember what happened to me and take care with your preparation.

Selling ideas and products

Recently I was involved in a one-on-one discussion with a young man who was going overseas on a mission to sell a product that he had just produced. He had read my best-selling book, *The Great Sales Book*, and had come to me to see if I could suggest anything that he could improve in his presentation. He had done a great job on his presentation so there was no need to add anything to it. The only other issue in my view was the understanding that his presentation would win or lose on the basis of his preparation. When we go to sell something, the sale is lost, or won, on the quality of our presentation, based on preparation. On his return he told me that he didn't know whether he was successful or not. The prospective buyers would meet to make a decision and convey their decision in a letter as soon as possible afterwards. His preparation was very good but on his return he rang me to give me details of his meeting with his prospective clients. Then he told me that even though the presentation had been excellent no decision was yet made. That, to me, was a sign that they would say no. He had come all the way from Australia but they weren't prepared to make a 'yes' decision. All the signs were 'no'.

On the road

When I am to make presentations in a number of different cities and towns, one of my constant worries is the possibility of an illness or accident that would make it impossible for me to perform. Promoters of tours have to spend a great deal of money upfront in terms of publicity, venue hire, speaking fees, accommodation, and so on. A cancellation would mean not only the loss of deposits and guarantees, but of all the promotion and sales material that has to be produced. The losses can be very substantial.

Only once in my 16 years on the professional speaking circuit have I been unable through illness to carry out a speaking assignment. Thankfully I was able to get a replacement speaker who I knew would do a first-class presentation.

The only time I have suffered any illness while on a tour was during a tour of New Zealand with Allan Pease, an authority on body language and communication. We had arranged the tour ourselves and were presenting on behalf of the New Zealand Institute of Management. Our first presentation was at Auckland approximately one hour after we arrived from Australia. By the end of my presentation I had a raging sore throat, my temperature was well up and the last thing I felt like doing was making a presentation for a couple of hours. Our next stop was in Christchurch so before leaving Auckland I went to see a doctor who gave me prescriptions and advised, 'Don't talk, for each time you do it will raise your temperature'. I hadn't told him that talking was my business and that I was there to do three two-hour talks. I took the medication and we went to Christchurch.

That afternoon we were to do a half-day seminar, of which I was to do two separate one-hour presentations and Allan would do the same.

On arriving at Christchurch I left the arrangements to Allan and went to bed because by that time I wasn't feeling so good. At 2.00 pm Allan did the first one-hour presentation and then I received a message: 'Get up and come and make a presentation'.

It was the most difficult presentation I have ever made in my whole life. Every word felt as if it was tearing my tonsils out and of course my temperature skyrocketed. I was feeling very ill, but when you're paid to do a presentation you don't want to let the audience know that you are suffering anything. From their point of view you need to look refreshed and do a first-class presentation and make them feel good.

As soon as I had finished that presentation I handed back to Allan and off I went to bed for another hour. When my time arrived it was out of bed, onto the podium and on with the show. I had to look as if I had just arrived from a week's holiday and make a brilliant presentation. Fortunately, all went well and all was well, except me.

Next day we had to go to Wellington and by that time the medication, especially the painkillers, had started to work and I was able to perform well without the major problems I had at Christchurch.

Adelaide conference

I was retained to be the keynote speaker at a motel franchise annual general conference in Adelaide. The group members had come from every state. The presentation they selected was 'Yes You Can', which is based on my book of the same name and must surely be the most asked-for presentation of its kind in Australia today. As I've mentioned, the presentation consists of three parts. The first part is about how to use the power of our mind to win in life and business. The second part is about time, because all things being equal, those who use their time to the best advantage will, in most cases, perform better than those who waste time. The third part is about setting and achieving goals. Almost everyone I know can set goals — that is the easy part. The hard part is the 'how to' of achieving the goals and that is a key part of my presentation.

The presentation ran for approximately three hours with breaks in between each session and the focus was on those who were present because the key issues are always about the people. Were they in fact using their minds, time and goals to their best advantage? Were they aiming for goals that were designed and organised to achieve their life objectives? The focus of the whole presentation was that we as individuals are in charge of these issues and we can design and use them, or we can ignore their importance and therefore create problems in our life and business.

During the presentation I made constant reference to whether or not what audience members were doing in their lives was in fact achieving what they most wanted. This is always a critical issue to every audience: many people are working against their own best interests, without realising it.

After the session was completed there was a 20-minute break and many people came and asked questions, seeking clarification on some issues and generally wanting to work out whether they were on the right track to get what they said was important to them. One woman came up and said, 'Well, Jack, you have solved a major problem for me.' I asked what the problem was and she said, 'The problem is simple. I was a matron in a hospital, I have two adult children, a boy and a girl, and I am a sole parent because my husband died. Believing I was doing the right thing I resigned from my position as matron and spent my savings and superannuation on buying a business so that my two children, aged 18 and 19, could have a business career. At that time, good positions were hard to come by.

'My great plan for my children didn't work out the way I had thought it would. Instead of them being involved in the business and anxious to grow the business and perhaps extend into a second one they showed not the least bit of interest, except on pay day. I've found that I am doing all the important work, taking all responsibility and my children appear quite happy to let me do so. They can be carefree, they have a good income and a boss who loves them and so from their point of view things couldn't be better.

'Today while I was listening to you I realised that I had made a major mistake in assuming that my children would become involved and grow the business for their own welfare. Because of the love of my children I have made a poor business decision, not in terms of the viability of the business, but because I am doing something I really don't want to do for myself. I have been doing it for my children, who apparently are not interested in running a business.

'Jack, tomorrow my children are going to get what I believe will be a temporary unpleasant surprise. As soon as I get back home I am going to put the business on the market and terminate the employment of both my children who will, God bless them, continue to love their mother. I will wish them the best of good luck in their search for a career for which they have to take all the responsibility. Jack, you have no idea how happy and relieved I am that today I have taken a decision which I should have made months ago, one I am sure is in the best interests of my children and certainly will improve the quality of my life. Thank you very much.' And with that, she put her arms around me and kissed me softly on the cheek. None of this surprised me. I have had many of these types of responses; they have made me feel that I am helping people create a better and happier life for themselves.

Christchurch conference

On one of my tours to New Zealand I was in Christchurch presenting a three-hour night-time public seminar on 'Yes You Can'. There were around 150 people present.

It has always been my practice when making a presentation to select at least one friendly face from the audience to check on whether at least one of the audience is reacting positively to what I am saying. In this case it was the warm and friendly face of a woman. She looked to be in her late fifties or early sixties. She had grey hair, a beautiful face and she was very interested in all parts of the presentation.

I was almost through the 'Mind' segment of the program when suddenly this woman started to cry. I couldn't help feeling that something I had said had upset her and while I continued talking I was trying to think of what it could possibly be. I did not want to embarrass her so I continued the presentation and at the end of the segment I called a 15-minute recess.

During the recess I took the opportunity to talk with her and asked her what it was that I had said that had reduced her to tears. She was embarrassed that this had happened and assured me that I had said nothing to upset or offend her. It was that she had been living with a problem she had not been able to resolve but during my presentation she became aware of what she must do to resolve it. She said that the relief of knowing she could resolve the problem broke down her resistance and she cried. She said, 'Jack, you will never know how much you have done for me by showing me the way to solve this problem. My life will be much better now that I don't have to live with that problem hanging over my head.'

At the conclusion of the evening's program several of the audience came up to me because they had seen me talking with the woman. They were concerned about her welfare and asked me if there was anything they could do to help. I assured them that there was now no problem and thanked them for their concern.

Just another incident in the life of a speaker, one that confirms that I am making some difference in the lives of many who come to my seminars. From the letters and phone calls I receive thanking me, I believe that many of my audiences get great benefit from the views I express and the way I present those views. Words have a great power and if used indiscriminately, can cause all sorts of problems. Great care needs to be taken and I never underestimate the power of words.

New Zealand

The story of the woman who reacted with tears leads me to a similar situation that I experienced during an evening seminar on selling techniques which I was conducting in New Zealand. At the time this incident occurred I was conducting a session called 'Questions are the Answer'. This session deals with the power of questions, with particular emphasis on using soft questions instead of hard questions. Hard questions result in the questioner getting a yes/no answer, while soft questions get more information. If we ask specific soft questions, such as Where, When, Which, What, Why, and How, we get more important information.

It is my practice during such a session to involve some of the audience in questions and answers to demonstrate how soft questions get more information. I generally select someone in the front row of the audience so that I can easily carry on a conversation with them, and so that the audience can hear that person's responses to my question they are given a hand-held microphone. Before I ask the question I do the best I can from observation to select someone in the audience who I believe will be able to participate with ease.

On this occasion I noticed a nice-looking young couple in front of me in the front row. They looked to be in their mid-twenties. I checked the woman's hand and she was wearing what appeared to be a wedding ring. Out of courtesy, I asked the young man, 'Are you married to the young lady on your left?' He said, 'Yes.' I then said to the audience, 'By asking a yes/no hard question I have a yes/no answer. In this case the answer is yes. If I had asked him a soft question I would have received more information, so I will now ask him a How question.' I turned to the young man and said 'How do you feel about being married?' To my astonishment he told everyone in the audience, 'The worst thing I ever did and as soon as I can get out of it I am away.' Well, the point was proved. If you ask soft questions you get more information. The young man was angry and the young woman was embarrassed, but they stayed on to the end and I continued on with the examples as if nothing untoward had happened. However, since then I have been very careful to ask questions about cars, or houses, or suburbs. I do not know if the couple resolved their problems but I learned one good lesson: don't ask questions that can get embarrassing answers.

From Bali to Perth

On one occasion I had been retained to make a major presentation at a conference at Bali which I had to give at 9.30 am for a period of two hours. I had been told that I could get a plane from Bali direct to Perth on the afternoon after I'd given my morning presentation in Bali. This was critical because I was also booked to do a half-day workshop at a major conference in Perth at 8.30 am on the following day.

On arriving at Bali I went to confirm my flight to Perth and found that the flight had been cancelled that day and there were no other direct flights to Perth. I was told that in order to get to Perth that night I would have to fly to Singapore and then get a direct flight around midnight from Singapore to Perth. The flight would arrive in Perth at 4.00 am. The plane from Bali to Singapore left at 1.30 pm and it was almost 12.30 before I could leave the conference venue so it was all rush and hurry. Fortunately the Singapore airport had motel type accommodation so I was able to snatch about four hours' sleep before the alarm said it was time to go.

I landed in Perth right on time. By the time I had disembarked, collected my luggage and made it to my hotel it was nearly 5 am so I unpacked, checked my slides and handouts, and made sure I was prepared to make my presentation, which was to be to a workshop of about 20 people. I had an hour thinking how good it would be to get some sleep and then it was time for breakfast and the conference. My workshop ran for the whole morning and by the end I was ready for some sleep! Fortunately, that type of time pressure is more the exception than the rule. The lesson I learned from this experience was to always be prepared to accept and overcome those unexpected changes to plans and be willing to deal with them in a positive manner.

Pacing myself

I had agreed with a promoter that I would do a tour of New Zealand for him based on the subject of my book *Yes You Can*. We agreed a price for each presentation plus expenses. The number of presentations and their location was left to the promoter. I was expecting that the presentation venues would be in Auckland, Wellington and Christchurch as the only information I had been given was that it would take me two days to complete the assignment.

I received a message to say the first presentation would be made in Auckland at 8.30 am on the day of my arrival. At 8.30 am I began my first presentation, a two-hour public seminar attended by around 350 people. The presentation went off well and I enjoyed a great reception. After the presentation I met with the promoter and his staff to be briefed on the rest of the tour. To my surprise I found that the promoter had booked me to make a two-hour presentation at Wellington at noon and then go on to Christchurch to do a public seminar on the same subject that evening at 8.00 pm. So on the first day I had done three two-hour presentations in the three major cities of New Zealand — and next morning we were to be back in Auckland for another presentation. When that was completed we drove to Rotorua to make a three-hour presentation starting at 8.00 pm that evening. Next morning we drove to Hamilton for another presentation and by early afternoon we were on our way back to Australia. I had made six major presentations in six different locations in two days. Never again. From then on I always made sure of what was happening and that I had not been overbooked.

Having the right equipment is critical

On two separate occasions I have had the same problem. No lectern for the speaker. It may well be possible to make a presentation from memory but I only did it once because the slide machine broke down. From then on I always spoke from written notes. Now I had the notes but no lectern. The building in which I was making the presentation had cost something like $200 million dollars to build and had just been opened. I was the keynote speaker at the first conference held in this new centre and no one had thought to buy a lectern. Everything else was first class. But no lectern — and I couldn't function without one.

I co-opted the help of one of the staff making the final preparations for the conference. The opening was in one hour and I was the principal speaker. She took me to the kitchen where I managed to get two milk crates and a cardboard beer carton. My helper borrowed a bed sheet from the linen room. After stacking the crates and carton one on each other, we covered them with the bed sheet, tied it around the stack and secured it with a red ribbon, tying a large red bow on the front of my now hand-made lectern. It looked okay from where the audience was sitting and I don't think they were any the wiser about our predicament.

The second time this happened to me, Allan Pease and myself were hired by a group who usually ran classical music shows in the town hall of a regional city. They had decided they would break with past practice and retain two motivators to run an evening on inspiration and motivation.

Allan and I were not too confident that we would have an audience, because those who went to classical music evenings were to our minds not likely to come to hear motivational speakers. The evening before the event the mayor of the city invited us to a function at which we received a very warm welcome to the city from all who attended. The question was still: would anyone turn up to hear our presentation?

The presentation was in the town hall. We arrived early to make sure the sound was okay. That we had pin-on mikes. That the screen for slides and the slide machine were all in working order. Everything was okay — except there was no lectern. An hour before the audience arrived and no lectern. Two cardboard boxes covered with a sheet soon solved the problem. As long as we didn't lean on the lectern, we were okay.

About 350 people turned up to hear our presentations, which was terrific. The audience was very responsive and the night went well.

Then came the problem. At the end of the presentations the mayor came onto the stage to thank us and the audience. Allan and I were sitting in the front row as he was making his thank-you speech. He was evidently a 'leaner-on-lecterns' speaker and before long he went to lean on the lectern. I said to Allan, 'If he leans on that lectern he will finish in your lap.' We were about one and a half metres below the lectern stage. Allan knew the mayor personally and for the next ten minutes every time he headed for the lectern Allan asked him a question which kept him at the front of the stage. Finally he finished and we climbed onto the stage and thanked him, standing between him and the lectern.

Hamilton Island

One of my favourite assignments was a presentation I made to a franchisee conference on Hamilton Island. The franchisors had selected time management and goal-achieving as the subject of my presentation. I was the last major speaker for that day and I had two hours in which to make my presentation to 80 franchisees. I selected 'Yes You Can' as the topic because it not only involved goal-achieving and time management but it also had a session on understanding self- and mind management. The audience was made up of almost equal numbers of men and women. They were a very responsive group and became involved in discussion whenever possible. As always, the audience wanted material that they could identify with at a human level because of course the more there is about human behaviour and interaction, the more the subject matter pertains to the audience.

When we came to the part dealing with our minds, the interest level rose and it really was a joy for me to see that so many of the audience were obviously anxious to know how they could use this information not only in a sales situation but in everyday life. All too soon the presentation was finished and the questions came thick and fast. The good news was that the audience was in harmony with the views I expressed and most wanted more information on how to use the techniques I discussed in their lives.

At the end, as the group was moving off, one woman came up and put her arms around me and shed tears on my shoulder. 'I am so sorry I am crying,' she said, 'but that was wonderful. It was about me — that's why I am crying. Thank you.'

Later on at lunch a young man of about 18 came up and said, 'Thank you. You were talking about me — it was wonderful.' So from one audience, a woman aged around 35 and a young man of around 18 were both telling me that what I was saying in the presentation was about them. The key to great presentations is that audience members feel the presentation is about them as an individual. When that happens, you know you have hit the mark.

I am ever amazed that my presentations can affect people to the extent that they shed tears. If a presentation affects people, it is because it taps into the human element in whatever subject is being presented. Life can be about strategies, techniques and tactics involved in business — whatever the business — but it is also always about the humans involved. Even when we are discussing products or services it is always about how they affect the humans involved. Every presentation is about humans, not only those taking part in the current session but humanity in a broader sense. All life is about people: how they feel about issues and how they are going to deal with them.

There are countless other audience response stories that I could relate; these are just a sample. Each presentation is a unique experience, both for myself and my audience.

7. Questions Are the Answer

Almost every presentation I have made can be divided into two broad categories: selling and management. If the presentation was about management it could have been on any of a number of management issues. If it was about sales it could have been about 'Making Powerful Sales Presentations' or 'The Hidden Buyer Motivators'. It could have been about 'Using Time Effectively' or 'Goal-achieving' if the audience was a mixture of both management and sales. In this case it is 'Questions are the Answer', which is about how to use soft questions to sell more effectively. Let me begin.

Mr Chairman, thank you for your kind welcome and for inviting me to make this presentation to your conference. The key subject today is 'Questions are the Answer'.

Let me begin the way I start most of my presentations. Some people die at 30, but aren't buried till 70. Here lies the mind of an individual who at the age of 30 or more has stopped thinking, is mentally dead and just waiting to be buried. I know this is not true of those who are here at this conference, but it is worth remembering it can happen to anyone at any time, unless they stay ahead of changes affecting us almost every day. Let me begin.

The sales climate in which we operate has changed significantly in the last decade in the following ways:

- Competition has increased dramatically.
- Time frames have shortened significantly.
- The community is generally better qualified than ever before in terms of understanding products and services.

Information for consumers is much more freely available now than at any other time in our history. This information comes from trade shows, exhibitions, product and services seminars, television specials, trade and services publications and a host of other media that is educating, instructing and directing the purchaser in our present economy. As a result of these and other changes in the perceived wants of the marketplace, selling presentations today need to be much more oriented to negotiation rather than confrontation. Today our selling objectives need to take account of the following techniques.

Ideas, concepts and philosophies

Selling ideas, concepts and philosophies is the easiest, most practical and effective way to ensure your success in today's marketplace. Ideas are about the product or the service and how it can be used in some special manner to benefit the prospect. Concepts are about how people feel; it is a soft sell, it's about them, it's about what they want from life for them and theirs. Philosophies are about us and how we feel, they are about what we believe is good and successful in life and why we believe our prospects could improve their chances by using some of our philosophy. Selling concepts and philosophies is about understanding the nature of the sales presentation, that it's a three-part process.

- Part 1 is the idea. The important part is to sell the idea before the solution. If they buy the idea you have made a sale.
- Part 2 is to sell yourselves. You are meant to sell the idea in a way that sells you at the same time. In most cases if they buy you, they will buy your funding and service. The more creative, exciting and emotive your idea, the more certain it is that they will buy you and your idea.
- Part 3 is to sell the funding. All ideas have to be funded. The real sale is to sell the idea, product or service. The funding backs up the idea. When they have bought the idea of how to get rich, the funding is the product or service that makes the idea work by producing the wealth that makes our prospect or client rich.

Those who sell products first limit their chances. Product and service is funding and it is a solution to the problem, or the satisfaction of the idea. Many salespeople are still selling the product. They go in with the product as step one and they can't understand why their prospect doesn't want to buy their product. The real reason is because the product is the solution and solutions are sold last, not first. For example, trying to sell a car to a prospect who has no transport problem is very difficult. Trying to sell a house to a prospect who does not have a housing problem is difficult. Trying to sell an investment product to someone who is already rich or who does not want to become rich is a problem. Selling advertising space to someone who does not believe in advertising is a problem. Once we understand that selling products and services is selling solutions we then understand the necessity of establishing the prospect's wants first, then the ideas and then solutions.

Sell wants, not needs. Almost everyone I know would like to be shown how to get what they want. Your prospect may need a four-bedroom, two-bathroom house but they want a three-bedroom, one-bathroom house. Your prospect may need a two-bedroom unit close to transport but your prospect wants a four-bedroom house with two bathrooms on two hectares remote from transport. The prospect may need a four-cylinder economy car but he wants a two-seater fire-eating sports car. Your prospects may need any one of 20 different solutions to their problem, but what they want is an entirely different matter. If what they need and what they want is the same thing, there are no difficulties. Whether you spend your time trying to convert people from what they want to what in your opinion they need is entirely up to you — but for my money, create and sell wants.

Use your skills in negotiation, not confrontation. Today in selling presentations there is a need for a lot of discussion, soft questions, and good questioning techniques instead of the virtual confrontation that exists when a salesperson decides to sell a product or service, come what may. Soft sell, not hard sell. By this I mean the iron fist in a velvet glove: the techniques of how to make presentations without appearing to be hard sell. There is a need, a great need, to learn these techniques and practise them at every sales presentation. Sell by using the power of soft questions — this is essentially what this program is about; questions and how they can help you have your prospects buy from you rather than you sell to them. In many cases, our prospect will buy from you if you help them establish and accept they have a problem they are willing to solve.

Many prospects will accept they have a problem but we only succeed when they are willing to solve it. We succeed in proportion to our ability to provide by way of a product or service a solution which is acceptable to our prospect. Selling has been described as being the art of solving problems; the truth is that it is the art of having prospects identify problems they are willing to solve.

Hard and soft questions

To discover what they want and how willing they are to solve their problem is easy if you ask the right questions: soft questions, attitude questions, feeling questions. Soft questions get information about what they think, what they believe in, what they want, what they are willing to do and how best they see themselves solving the problem.

Hard questions are about facts and and have little or nothing to do with how our prospects feel, nothing to do with their attitudes. Hard questions require no real involvement on the part of the prospect. If you continue to ask hard questions it is really a one-way communication process. Hard questions ask: How old are you? How much life insurance do you have? Are you married? Where do you live? How much do you spend on advertising? What type of car do you drive? How much income do you earn? This is all information which can be put to good use but nonetheless, having asked all our questions, we really know very little about our prospect. We know nothing of how our prospect feels, what our prospect thinks, what our prospect wants, what our prospect likes, or dislikes. All of this information only comes when we ask soft questions.

The soft questions we are most often going to ask are the seven W's — Who, What, When, Where, Why, Which, Would — plus How. The most powerful of these are How and Why. Most of the questions we ask will begin with one of these words. How we use the words depends on how we ask the questions. We ask the questions to get answers. And in order to know what questions to ask we need to know what answers we want.

You are looking for answers that will tell you how your prospect feels about what you are presenting, so you ask questions to find out. For example, if you are selling money, you want to know how your prospect feels about getting rich. A hard question: 'How old are you?' Answer: '45.' Soft question: 'How do you feel about being 45?' If you receive a non-committal answer such as 'Good' then continue with soft questions. 'What makes you feel good about being 45?' If the answer is a non-committal 'I feel good about being 45 because I am not 60', continue with a soft question. 'What makes you feel badly about being 60?' The technique is to keep asking soft, non-threatening questions until your prospect is encouraged to start giving you feelings, attitudes, beliefs, desires.

More examples — hard question: 'Are you married?' Answer: 'Yes.' Soft question: 'How do you feel about being married?' If you get a non-committal answer, simply extend the soft questions by asking, 'Why do you feel that way?'

More hard questions. 'What type of car do you own?' He gives you the model and make. Now that you understand the car, ask the real question: 'How do you feel about your present car?' You might like to ask, 'What could you improve about your present car?' Or, 'What do you not like about your present car?' But when you ask specific questions like that you get the answer to only one area of attitudes and feelings. If you ask, 'How do you feel about your present car?' you may get a lot of answers that you would not have received by asking more specific soft questions. Hard question: 'What type of house do you live in?' Soft question: 'How do you feel about your present house?' Hard question: 'Where do you live now?' Soft question: 'How do you feel about living in your present locality?' Hard question: 'How much do you spend on your current advertising?' By asking this type of question you get dollars and you get the limits of their thinking at the moment but little else. Perhaps it would be better to ask a soft question such as, 'What is your philosophy on advertising?' Hard questions are final and give us little or no ongoing dialogue. We are finished unless we ask soft questions. Answers to soft questions tell us what we need to know to make a sale. We discover wants. We identify solutions and we begin to understand how our prospect feels about what we are talking about.

If you are selling investment real estate you want to know how your prospect feels about investment in real estate, or if the answer is not favourable, ask another soft question: 'Why do you feel investment in real estate is not a favourable investment for you?' If you are selling advertising you want to know how your prospect feels about buying advertising so you ask this soft question: 'How do you feel about advertising?' or 'What is your philosophy on advertising?' If the answer is not favourable you need to know why, so you ask why. If you are selling money, you want to know how your prospect feels about getting rich. If the response is favourable you still have to find which of the available options they favour. For instance, banks, shares, building societies, credit unions, trusts or the property sector. Perhaps some of each. If your prospect doesn't favour your product or service you need to find out why, and so you ask a 'why' soft question.

No matter what you sell, you want to know how your prospect feels, what they believe and what they want. Sometimes we simply want an alternative so we're asked an alternative question, for instance, 'Would you prefer to pay cash or charge it?', 'Would you prefer to pay yearly or monthly?', 'Would you prefer red or yellow?', 'When would you like to travel, this week or next week?', 'Mondays or Fridays?', 'What size would you prefer, large or small?' These questions tell you your prospect's preference but they don't tell you how they feel, or why they prefer that option. Constructive questioning can soon bring out all the key information you need in order to offer a solution to the identified problem.

Questions, questions, questions. Asking questions is futile unless you listen to and understand the answers. Whether you agree or disagree, believe or don't believe is not the issue, you have your answer. You may not like your answer, but it is their answer, it's their life, their beliefs, their feelings, their money and it's their problem. Listen attentively. Keep quiet while they decide on their problem and their solution. Just keep posing soft questions to help them get the answer to their problem. When you get their answer, you only have to provide the funding and the sale is complete.

Some don'ts

Don't interrupt. Listen and when they have finished answering your question and you need more or different information then enlarge or rephrase your question, but only when they have finished the answer to your first question.

Don't answer your own questions. Many salespeople continually answer their own questions. By doing this they restrict their prospect to yes-and-no answers, which defeats the purpose of asking open-ended questions.

Don't criticise your prospect's choices. Work around them by asking selective questions which will expose any weaknesses in their choices which they may have overlooked. If your sales presentation style depends on getting a particular answer to your questions then it is better to make statements and seek agreement than to ask questions and provide the answers.

Some do's

Explore options. Your prospects will always have options so get them out in the open where they are not likely to become a hidden objection. You can do this by simply asking soft questions such as, 'How do you see yourselves achieving your goal?' Wait for the answer. Then ask another soft question, 'What, in your opinion, are the alternatives?' Wait for the answer. Ask another soft question: 'Which do you favour and why?' Wait for the answer, and if your alternative is not included, ask another question: 'Why did you not include . . .?' and then identify your alternative. By now you know where you stand, if your option does not rank highly you have more work to do. Don't criticise their choices; that only builds resistance. Your only real alternative is to build the benefits of your option until they exceed your prospect's choices.

Emphasise the problem. Spend 80 per cent of your time on the problem and 20 per cent on the solution. Once your prospect accepts the problem and shows a willingness to solve it, the sale is made. The solution only completes the process. If you have a satisfactory solution the sale is yours.

To keep our questions in sequence and use them in the right order their use needs to be matched to the sales track we are using. If we are organised, we have a sales track. If not, we do our best by matching our wits with those of our prospect. Matching wits soon turns into a contest. In contests someone generally loses and too often it is the salesperson. So be well organised, have a sales track and a good one.

For our purpose we will use AIDA

A — Attention
I — Interest
D — Desire
A — Action

In the 'attention' part of the sales track we can quite effectively substitute strong attention-gripping statements, or we can use powerful questions designed to get attention. This program is not about selling techniques so we will not go further into the matter of getting attention, except to say that research shows us that 75 per cent of all sales presentation failures occur in the attention phase. So designing strong, powerful statements and questions is important.

Most of your prospect's questions will relate to the interest–desire–action part of your sales presentation. Many salespeople have said that if they could only make their prospect want what they are selling as easily as they know how to tell him what they are selling, then they would have it made. Attempts to discover successful methods for arousing this want have usually been confusing. For example, one author suggests: 'Arouse your prospect's desire with a few well-chosen words'. Question: what well-chosen words? It is not possible to tell in advance what those words should be. They have to be well-chosen but in relation to what? They need to be well-chosen in relation to what it is that you perceive your prospect will respond to. You have to keep looking. You have to find what motivates your prospect. You have to detect their hidden motive. When you get to this phase of a sales presentation, you're dealing with the emotional human being and this is where you discover your prospect's real desire, if you are to make the sale. You need to know as much as is possible about your prospect before you go to the selling interview and this can only be achieved by specific research. Being well prepared in terms of knowing about your prospect before you go to the interview is not always possible, so in that case your questioning technique needs to be non-threatening. You should, as best you can, be interesting in what you say and that will become more apparent as you continue your questioning.

To motivate your prospect to buy, you must detect his or her hidden dominant buying urge and then find a way to answer or satisfy that urge. Use the power of soft questions. Ask them in a soft, non-threatening way. Prospects don't just want to save money, they want to save money for a reason, or more than one specific reason. It may be to travel, to buy a larger home, or to buy a bigger or different car, or maybe just to win the approval of friends and neighbours. The only real way that we can find the hidden dominant buying urge of our prospect is to ask related questions and listen for the answers so that we get the clues about their primary drive, or impulse, that creates the 'action' for them to buy. Our prospect is like us. We act because we want or need something. We need to ask soft questions about how our prospect feels, in order to determine their attitude and to find out what our prospect really wants. Then we can show them how we can help them get what they want. Many of you will say, 'Yes, I know all this', but knowing isn't doing. The real issue is: do you do it? Not just now and again but always? I hope I have managed to convey to you that soft questions are the way to sales success and I wish you well in your future selling career.

8. Turning Yourself on to Success

This half-day presentation is one of the most popular of all my presentations because it is a key issue for any who want to achieve outstanding success. You can't buy success in a supermarket. You can't rent it from any provider. You can't achieve much without it and if you want it you have to provide it yourself. So go for it with every talent at your disposal. Don't wait, opportunity is knocking and it may be too late tomorrow. We should follow Theodore Roosevelt's advice when he said, 'Far better it is to dare mighty things, to win glorious triumphs even though checkered by failure, than to rank with those poor spirits who neither enjoy nor suffer much because they live in the gray twilight that knows neither victory nor defeat.' At the end of this presentation is an interview with my friend Greg Nathan, who is a psychologist, an author and a very successful businessman. His practical attitude to life's problems and desires have always impressed me as advice worth following.

Mr Chairman, thank you for your invitation to be here today. Let me begin by saying that some people die at 30 but aren't buried till 70. Here lies the mind of an individual who at whatever age has stopped thinking, is mentally dead and just waiting to be buried. Now I don't think that description fits any of you here today, but if we are not careful we can easily fall into a rut that becomes a permanent way of thinking that is less than helpful. My presentation is 'Turning Yourself on to Success'. Let me begin.

Suddenly we are being engulfed by change, not because we wanted it but because we have been resisting it for generations and now the floodgates have opened and a new world is being born. Drucker's global village and information society is now a reality. The marriage of communications and computers has opened the world to anyone with technology. Barriers that have stood for centuries have been smashed. Censorship is now almost impossible. The power of countries is being altered. Financial markets are at the mercy of the traders. Executive power is severely depleted. Top managers no longer own the big picture. Management layers have disappeared and international trade has become more difficult.

These are the changes that are causing concern to humans all over the world. The long-term security and certainty that we hunger for in our lives has been disappearing with these changes. Job uncertainty, longer hours and less time with family are all taking their toll. These concerns arise because the environment in which we work and live is changing faster than we humans want to adapt. The basic nature of humans has not changed significantly over thousands of years, perhaps millions. The fundamentals of human emotions are the same. We still desire things for the same reasons. We still resist ideas for the same reasons. We still love, fear, hate, envy, succeed, fail and persist for the same reasons as we have over thousands of years. No amount of change is going to alter that in any way that is likely to affect you in your pursuit of your key goals. Whatever you do, do not confuse the issue of technology with basic human emotions, or you will limit your success. Technology can make us more effective but never forget that in the end it's our human emotional responses to technology that will decide its future and the future of the individuals who use it.

All motivation is self-motivation

Others can inspire us in a way that causes us to become self-motivated and as a result we make plans and take action designed to achieve a particular goal. When we lie down in a heap, full of despair and worry, we are totally motivated to lie down in a heap, full of despair and worry. Self-motivation is the quality you need to foster if you want to reach your goal of becoming successful in all your endeavours, especially the goal of achieving financial independence by creating wealth in your life. It is your goal and you need to build the motivation within yourselves so that you will become committed to reaching it. What can you do to motivate yourself to take action towards creating wealth in your life?

As the chief motivator of 'You Yourselves Incorporated' you have the task in your life of keeping at a high level your will and desire to succeed. Unless you pay attention to what you want nothing much will happen in this important part of your life. If you focus on the issues and develop specific goals to achieve your objective, you will have done much of what needs to be done in terms of self-motivation. Why is it so important? Because, as US aircraft businessman Norman Augustine said, 'Motivation will almost always beat mere talent.' Self-development is a critical issue in all our lives. It is not something we do now and again if we want to be successful, it is something we need to do all the time. It is not something separate from us, it is our life, it is the way we live. You Yourselves Incorporated can become a run-down, worn-out, tired and neglected entity, or it can be a dynamic, enthusiastic, growing, wealthy and successful one: the choice is entirely up to you. After all, it is your goal and your life and if you value your goal enough you will create the motivation within yourselves to act.

All life is an expansion. It's a learning process from birth to death. Every day we are confronted with the necessity to learn and grow and those who embrace the opportunities instead of resisting them make the swiftest progress.

Once you respond to self-development you draw more opportunities to yourselves and you build your motivation. You are master of your own destiny. The cold hard facts of human development are that it is all self-development. You're the managing director, marketing manager, sales manager, accountant, designer, advertising manager, investment manager and, above all else, the chief motivator of You Yourselves Incorporated. You are your greatest asset, irrespective of the current level of your expertise. The more you hone, polish and shape your capacity in your chosen field the more you are worth on the open market. When you can do more and are willing to do more, you will be worth more.

Why is it that some people are paid hundreds, sometimes thousands of dollars an hour while others are paid twenty dollars an hour? To make sure you join the group of highly paid individuals you need to be a creative thinker and search constantly for new and innovative ways to perform your work so that you are building a reputation not only for being good at what you do but for being different. Just as businesses need to differentiate themselves from their competitors you need to do the same in your field of expertise.

Building motivation

You should constantly be focusing on the following issues in order to build your motivation and work towards your goal.

- Focus all your efforts towards achieving the goal of becoming a totally motivated individual.
- Direct your behaviour towards developing attitudes and habits that raise your motivation and increase your overall ability and chances of success.
- Study until you become an expert in the key issues of your chosen field of work.
- Direct your own time management so that you can meet and exceed the requirements of your work.
- Earn the reputation of being one step ahead of your opposition.
- Direct yourselves in a positive, helpful way and you will achieve increased motivation and confidence and your self-esteem will grow. You will find that you are not only building a first-class reputation, but also a different, new, highly motivated and exciting you.

As the chief of You Yourselves Incorporated you should develop a network of people who are already successful in areas that you want to develop in your life. Remember there are three factors that will decide much of the success you achieve in your life. They are what you see, what you hear and who you associate with. The choices are always up to you. If you want You Yourselves Incorporated to thrive, then make choices that will help you build it into what you want it to be.

Leadership and you

This is a quality you have to earn by what you do. Leadership is not bestowed upon anyone. It is earned by performance. Leaders in any field are followed and you can display leadership qualities by the way you perform your work and by the example you set to everyone you come in contact with. Great leaders are highly self-motivated individuals who will endure hard work and setbacks because they recognise that success does not always come easily and they are willing to pay the price that such success demands. That legendary leader of people, Vince Lombardi said, 'It is time for us all to stand and cheer for the doer, the achiever — the one who recognises the challenge and does something about it.' How right he was — and the ones who should cheer loudest are yourselves, for yourselves, because the way you see yourselves is critical to your self-performance and motivation. Set yourselves high performance objectives, then go after them with purpose and passion. Be proud of your ability to outperform your organisation's expectations of you. When you do, your reputation grows and great success follows. It's your career you are building and you are the one who will get the benefits. If you are self-employed the advice is the same. Great businesses are built by passionate, highly self-motivated people who draw similar people to them as employees and collectively they win.

Focus on the future, not the past

Focus on why an idea will work, not on why it won't. Focus on results, not the process. When you develop this positive, can-do type of thinking and motivation, not only will you raise your own levels of commitment and confidence but your attitude will rub off on others. Then you will get the benefit of their enthusiasm and determination and you will mark yourselves as a leader. Not only will your ability and confidence rise but so will your income.

Develop within yourselves leadership characteristics

Can you think of any other time when leadership qualities in all sections of the community were more desperately needed? If we look at leadership in terms of the acceptance by all kinds of organisations that the only real resource they have is the intellectual capacity of the people who make up their organisation, then our objective must be to perform at the highest level. Whatever your role and capacity, whether you are employed by an organisation or running your own business, you need to help those who work with you to achieve their true potential in terms of intellectual capacity. We are reaching a time in our development when the success of our organisations will be decided by the intellectual capacity of their people. As CPA Australia has said, the only true asset of any business is its human resource. Having outstanding intellectual ability is one thing, doing something worthwhile with it is another. Irrespective of your talent, the factor that drives you to use that talent to its full is self-motivation. To enjoy continual, outstanding success you need to develop your talent, and at the same time you need to motivate yourself to the highest possible level. When Muhammad Ali said, 'Champions are made of something deep inside them — a desire, a dream, a vision', he knew it to be true, for he had that desire, vision and dream and he went after it and made it true in his life. The same applies to you in your dream of achieving success and financial independence. When you go after it with determination, passion and every skill at your disposal, nothing can hold you back from achieving your goal. Go for it!

The right goals

When individuals feel demotivated, they are simply acknowledging that they aren't directing their activities towards achieving what is important to them, or they are working hard but either getting no real results or feel the results aren't worth the effort. Each of us needs to know how to get what we want. Often, the reason we don't perform is because we don't know the rules, or because we know the rules but don't follow them. Your objective should be to direct your motivation towards those things most likely to get you what you want out of life and your work. This can only be done if your motivation is directed by goals that you believe in, that will help you to achieve the things you really want.

Developing a positive self-image

Self-image is the factor which limits your performance in life. As you see yourselves, so you act. It is impossible to consistently perform at a higher level than your current self-image. If you want to improve your performance, become a more positive person and be more in charge of your life, then you need to improve your self-image so that you can see yourselves doing and achieving the things you want. Much of your self-image has been developed by interpreting the reactions of others to what you do and who you are and that's the reason why many of us suffer from fears and insecurities. I have never known a top-class successful person who didn't have a healthy self-image. They believe they are people of value who are doing something of value, and they rarely take rejection personally. Rather, they see it as being about what they are doing rather than about them personally. So it is very important to ensure that the problems you have in your daily life aren't the results of a low self-image.

If you want to improve your current self-image you can do so by using your self-talk to send the right messages to your subconscious mind. This unconscious mind cannot tell reality from illusion, or fact from fiction, so one of the first things you need to do is to act as if you are already in possession of the high self-esteem you would like. You need to visualise yourselves as a capable, confident person going about your business and life in a confident manner. You need to see yourselves as a valuable human being, someone worth loving, worth respecting and worth knowing. Each day as you act out your new-found confidence and continue to visualise yourselves as being the person you would like to become, you are in effect building that person. Each day, if you stick at it, you will get a little closer to your goal and finally the change will have been accomplished and you will have become the person you have been practising to be.

Reward yourselves for doing well

If you were given the task of motivating a particular person, one of the first things you might do would be to set up a reward system for high performance. It could be a money bonus, time off, a week away at a special place, or a meal at a special restaurant. All of these rewards are a good form of motivation. If you would do this for someone else, why not do it for yourselves? Pay yourselves, even if your organisation also pays you. Give yourselves some real incentives to perform. Set up daily and weekly goals and decide what reward you will pay yourself if you succeed. Remember, it is you who is doing the work and superior performance deserves to be rewarded.

Praise yourselves

You would certainly praise superior performance to enhance team motivation, so why not praise yourselves when you perform at a superior level? It's easy to focus on what you should have done, rather than praise yourself for what you actually did. It's okay to praise yourself when you have earned the praise. Don't be embarrassed; you're the only person hearing your praise, so don't hold back. Always follow the golden rule of giving praise as soon after the event as possible. The more praise you give yourself, the more likely you will perform at a superior level and the more likely you are to repeat the performance. What we think about ourselves is a critical factor in driving us on to greater accomplishment. In the words of my friend Denis Waitley, 'It's not what you are that holds you back, it's what you think you're not.' Denis is a recognised master motivator, an expert on personal development and a best-selling author. Focus on building on the qualities you have and remember you are always better than you think you are.

Strike failure from your vocabulary

The words 'failure' and 'I tried' are judgemental. There is rarely a total failure or a total success. If you don't achieve a goal, see it as a need to try again rather than as a failure. There are very few first-time total successes or total failures. Build on what was good and try again. Recently, a man who had been buying Lotto tickets for many years won in excess of $2 million. When asked about how he had succeeded he said: 'I've been playing Lotto for 17 years and have never changed the numbers. I believed that sooner or later they would come up.' But Lotto is not life and life is not Lotto! The rules and conditions about life are always changing. What won last year may be this year's big loser and the quality that separates winners from losers is always judgement. If you give away concepts of failure and losing, with all their value judgements, and focus on the positive news, you will enhance your chances of success enormously. You will increase your motivation, raise your positive expectations and in a short time, you will become what you have focused on: positive, motivated and successful.

How often do we hear the words, 'I tried, but it didn't work'? For too many people, 'trying' absolves them from facing up to one of life's great truths, which is that we either did or didn't achieve what we set out to do.

If you focus on doing instead of trying, two things will happen. First, you will succeed more often, because doing is more positive than trying. Second, because you will have removed the failure syndrome, your motivation will improve until you find yourselves expecting to succeed, and the expectation of winning is the result of a positive, 'I can win' self-image. Very few people are totally successful. No matter what level you are performing at, it is always a case of *I did*, or *I didn't*. Use the *I did* occasions to build confidence and the *I didn't* ones to learn how to improve, so that next time the possibilities of success are increased.

Nothing succeeds like success, so if it is necessary to tackle less difficult goals in order to achieve some positive successes, do so. It is better to have a realistic target and achieve it, than one that is beyond you and which hinders your self-confidence and becomes a self-fulfilling prophecy of defeat. Once you have established some successes, move the target up and it won't be long before you will be wondering why targets were a problem. Knowing how to motivate yourselves is the key issue in improving and maintaining your performance. Getting things done is what brings the rewards and in order to get things done you must be committed to the task in question. Without strong commitment it is easy to lapse into old habits and your drive disappears.

How to increase your motivation

Set your goal. Make it your dream. Hold it constantly in your mind. Keep repeating to yourselves, '*I am success, I am success, wealth, health and happiness will flow to me in abundance, I am success*'. Read, plan and live success. Focus on the positive, what you want, not on what you want to avoid. See your dreams coming true. Hold visions of success constantly in your mind. Remember, what the mind can conceive the mind can achieve. Focus on results, not the process. The winners are those who expect to win, so join the club. Here is what Kieren Perkins at the Atlanta Olympics had to say when he stormed back from dismal form to win the men's 1500-metre freestyle:

> *I visualised exactly what was going to happen tonight. It's hard to explain, but when you are focused, you almost have no thought. Sitting behind the blocks I was 100 per cent focused and I didn't have a single thing in my mind. I got in there, I knew what I had to do and it was just a matter of letting my instincts take over.*

Kieren was not only a world champion swimmer but he has always been a great role model for those who want to excel and do better. He is constantly working with people to help them reach their goals in life. Set yourselves high performance objectives and go after them with every talent you have.

The positive outcomes of self-motivation

All motivation is self-motivation. The inspiration to motivate ourselves can come from many sources but if we do not develop self-motivation, nothing happens. That is why this subject is so important to each of us. When you master self-motivation everything is possible.

- Once you have it the world opens up to you in a way that may now seem impossible.
- Your focus will be on self-development as a way to really understanding self-motivation because the desire to succeed in any endeavour will fail without sufficient drive and purpose.
- With positive self-motivation you can become a dynamic, enthusiastic, growing, wealthy and successful individual driven by the motivation to excel and achieve your goals.
- You can become master of your own destiny, no longer relying on chance for your success.
- You will focus on the future, not the past, for the future has all you want, the past has nothing more to give.
- You will understand that self-praise is essential to developing self-motivation as long as it is based on self-achievement that deserves recognition and praise.

- You will develop the positive habit of focusing only on what you want to achieve, not on what you want to avoid, and on results, not process.
- When developing your goals you will focus on achievable goals, not on those that are more a wish than a desire.
- Commitment to your goals will be what drives you to outstanding performance. Nothing too difficult. Nothing too hard.
- The winner's way will be yours because your mind-set will be on achieving, not wishing or hoping.

The need for lifelong education

We can be certain of four issues about the future. The first is that it will be a time of great uncertainty. The second is that it will be very different from today. The third is that the difference will come at an ever-increasing pace. The fourth is that we need to become lifelong learners. Other probable outcomes of these changes are that the knowledge workers of today and the future will need to be constantly topping up their specialities, and at longer intervals will need complete education refresher courses in the basics of their particular work. From now on we all need to become lifelong learners, firstly because those who cannot, or will not learn, will become the new poor of our society and secondly because today's knowledge can swiftly become obsolete if it is not constantly updated.

The greatest asset in any organisation today is the intellectual capacity of its people. Individuals will need to constantly improve their intellectual capacity and worth to their employer who, in many cases, will more than likely be themselves. In this new world of constant and ever-quickening change each of us must take responsibility for our own futures and lifelong education. We can no longer assume we only need to acquire a skill and that will be enough. Skills don't change that much but the knowledge that underpins them does and it is knowledge that is the key need in business today.

The key issue about knowledge is that it is transferable. It belongs to those who have it, not those who employ it. It is mobile, it shifts with the person. It is an individual's marketable asset and the more it is honed and perfected the more valuable it becomes. It only loses value when it is not kept up to date. It is more valuable the more creatively it is used. Diversity of information and knowledge is becoming critical to the success chances of the individual who by now is usually aware that a lifelong career with one organisation is no longer a real possibility. The life span of a successful organisation is limited and is ever shortening, as are the success chances of the individual who fails to become a lifelong learner.

A crucial success strategy for the individual is to firstly accept that knowledge is the currency of today; it is money in the bank — and it is your bank. In the future if you want to increase the value of your knowledge, you must constantly update and extend it so that you become a more marketable, valuable and innovative knowledge worker. Each of us has the capacity to increase our value by increasing our knowledge. In this new society it is the only way. The greater your knowledge, the better your chances — provided you know how to make that knowledge productive.

Three life issues that will affect every human being

What we see

If we take each day as it comes without stopping to critically examine how what we see is affecting our life, then to a certain extent we are travelling blind. For the next 14 days, take notice of what is happening in your life and ask yourself, 'Is this the result of what I am seeing and in many cases choosing to see?' Then ask yourself, 'Is it affecting me for good, or is it building what I would not wish to have happen in my life?' In most cases what you see will be a revelation because it is a critical factor in how your life is unfolding. The solution is to firstly get a clear picture of what is happening in your life and then ask yourself, 'Do I have control over what I see?' The answer will probably be yes.

You can control what you read and if you find you are mostly reading books and articles that contain little of what is educational, or challenging, then you should become more selective. Read books that will build your character and add to the knowledge that you need in order to become exceptional in your work and life. Will what you read be about successful and happy people who have made their mark in the world, or will it be about those who have made no real contribution to society except to reinforce all that is against its norms? There is a saying, 'Tell me what you read and I will tell you what you think and who you are trying to become.'

Will the same go for television and films? Will you seek out films that challenge your thinking, that have a message that is helpful in developing your character, or will you favour those that have no real message but just pander to popular opinion? Remember, the choices you make are building — or destroying — your plans to become exceptional. Always focus your attention on what will build a life of happiness and achievement. Always move towards what you want to become and away from that which you do not want to become. It is so easy to give way to those things that bring instant gratification, but do little, or nothing, towards you becoming exceptional. Life is not always easy. The choices we have to make to build an exceptional life are often difficult but the outcome of becoming exceptional is full of satisfaction and joy. You will have no personal recriminations if you set your goal and achieve it despite the difficulties that will no doubt come your way.

What we hear

Will you wander casually through life content only if what happens to you is easy and pleasurable? Will you choose to hear what is popular and gratifying, or will you make the decision to focus on what will build you a life of satisfaction and achievement? Once you choose to become exceptional you have chosen a path that is not trodden by the mob. You have now decided to become a member of a much smaller group, for whom challenge and the joy of personal achievement is the reward for becoming exceptional. Remember, few tread this path because it is a path of discipline and constant personal development. Will you seek out people who know more of what you want to know and who will help you on your way to becoming exceptional? Will you join an organisation that has these goals for its members and that will bring you speakers who will deal with issues you want to master? Remember, school is never out for those who want to become exceptional. It is a lifetime journey, for there is a constant need to keep up. If you give up, you will soon fall behind and your goal will be lost.

Who we associate with

This is a critical issue for all of us because it is a very public decision. Most of us will be judged by who we associate with. It is said that, 'birds of a feather flock together' and that 'like begets like'. That is how the public thinks. If you choose to be one who follows the most popular trends you will soon get lost among the masses. If you want to be your own person, you need to be capable of saying 'No' even when you know that 'No' will make you different to the crowd and the crowd will put pressure on you to conform.

This is where you win or lose in this particular part of your life. If you choose the popular route, the one chosen by most others, you lose. Why? Because the popular is the easy road; it takes no courage to join a mob. When you say 'No' to the greater majority who make up the largest crowd, you will have joined a smaller crowd who are made up of people who are more individualistic. Your attitude will be appreciated. When you belong to this group you then stand a better chance of learning what you need to know about successfully building your life.

These choices about building a successful and happy life are not easy; they take courage and discipline, but no matter what age or stage of development you are in building your life, if you want to reach the top in terms of success it is within your grasp now — provided you know what you want to achieve. When you were born you were given a life, not a life sentence. Life for each of us is a forever unfolding, challenging and growing opportunity, but the price is never decided in advance and is never paid in money. It is paid in commitment, effort, decisions, happiness and at times heartbreak and always there is the need to adapt to changing circumstances over which we often have little or no control. None of these issues are in themselves life-destroyers if we place our trust in the power greater than ourselves. When I was 31 I had a heart attack and spent two months in bed recovering. We lost a business and had to start again. Life unfolded in one continuous flow of success that is still happening. Perhaps the power knew what was best for me and changed our direction? Perhaps it sees the ways to better and happier times which we do not see and in order to bring them to our attention it creates circumstances that let us see the light and the opportunity. I know from experience, because I have been there.

There is no prize for becoming a lifelong, highly self-motivated individual, other than the satisfaction and the rewards that your efforts will bring and the knowledge that you are performing to the best of your ability. In the end it is this knowledge — that you did the best you could, not only to improve your own life, but to influence for good the life of many others to whom you will have become a role model. That is the icing on the cake of life.

Thank you for having me at your conference. I have enjoyed every minute of making this presentation. I wish you well and may you enjoy every success in developing and using innovation in the future.

The following extract is from an interview with psychologist Greg Nathan in which I asked him how we can develop happiness and contentment in our lives.

Greg, in your work as a psychologist what do you consider to be the main issue people need to resolve in their life to develop happiness within themselves?

Jack, contentment is an easy word to say — but it's not all that easy to practise. I say this because the practice of contentment is one of the keys to happiness and a truly happy person is not a common sight. If we take a little time to slow down and appreciate what we have and what is good in our lives I am sure this would be helpful. Often people get themselves worked up because things are not the way they think they should be. They say it's not fair that their life is unfolding in a particular direction. It seems to me that it is these unmet expectations that cause our unhappiness. Often we make a judgement as to whether something is fair or not fair based on our own limited time frame of thinking, but of course there is always a bigger picture. We need to allow time for things to unfold in their own way and in their own time. Who knows what's good, or not good in the bigger scheme of things or in the longer term? You may be disappointed that you missed out on a seat at a concert. Who knows you may have been badly maimed in a car accident if you had travelled to the concert on that particular night. Better to accept what is and to make the most of it. I guess this does take a certain amount of faith, which some people seem to find easier than others.

Greg, how best can people develop strong personal motivation within themselves?

Most people I know who have had this inner motivation have suffered humiliation or disappointment. Somehow this has triggered a defiance within them to say, 'I am not going to let this happen again. I am going to do something about this.' In a sense this is a very positive and creative way to turn defeat into victory. In fact, most people who I admire because of their drive and persistence have a story to tell. Just ask anyone who is powering ahead in their life why it is so important to them and I am sure you will hear something of a very interesting and touching nature. In a sense this is related to what I mentioned earlier about having faith that there is a bigger picture to things beyond our short-term suffering or disappointment. Often it is these very things that are shaping us to become more powerful and contributive than if things always went according to our own convenient, small-minded plans.

Greg, how best can people develop self-worth in their life?

Funnily enough, self-worth comes when we let go of trying to impress other people. I have found that when I am focused on a goal that is meaningful to me or when I say what I truly believe to be true, this is when people seem to respond well to me. On the other hand, when I try to impress others I become less myself, in a sense a weaker person. So the best way to develop self-worth is to do things that we believe are important. This means that we need to retain a sense of purpose in every situation we find ourselves. I find that the simplest and most effective way to do this is to look around and ask myself, 'How can I be helpful in this situation?' Not to impress anyone or to be liked. Just to be useful and to act with a purpose. This type of thinking focuses the mind in a positive way and builds self-worth. Some people would call it being of service. I would call it not being a waste of space. One other thing that helps build self-worth is self-discipline. Somehow this strengthens the will and gives us a greater sense of personal power. If someone were to combine the things we have talked about so far, that is, practising contentment, or being helpful and introducing some simple disciplines into their lives, I think they would be a very positive person.

Greg, so many people today seem to be concentrating on wealth as a source of happiness. Would you care to express an opinion about this issue?

This makes me a bit sad and maybe even a bit guilty because I worked for many years in the field of marketing. Despite all the rhetoric about marketing being about meeting people's needs, it is really about creating fuel for our consumer society. Marketing fuels demand which creates consumption and to consume we need wealth. If we were honest, people really only need five things: air, water, nutritious food, shelter and love. The rest is icing on the proverbial cake. Unfortunately money often tends to make people greedy and selfish. This may raise the hackles of some people who preach that you can have anything you want in life. This is possibly true, but I do not see wealth as a source of happiness. You might have a more comfortable lifestyle if you have more money; this does not mean you will have less stress, or less worries because these things are created by the mind. Many wealthy people suffer from depression and many less wealthy people are very happy, provided they have the basics I referred to above. Unfortunately it's the love that's missing in the lives of many. Although we chase wealth believing it will bring us love, it just doesn't deliver. If anything wealth creates fear and jealousy. I don't mean to be a party-pooper on this one. There is nothing wrong with having money. It's the chasing of it in the belief that it will answer some deeper meaning in our life that I am challenging.

9. It's About Time

I have made this presentation at least 50 times because it is one of the most frequently requested. Using time effectively is a major problem that most people have to contend with in their business and social lives. The issue of time is usually described as 'time management'. The problem is that it is impossible to manage time. If you don't believe that statement: stop the clock. We have had enough time today; let's have 30 hours tomorrow instead of 24. You can't do that? Of course you can't, because time is a non-manageable resource. You are going to get it whether you want it or not. The only way you can stop time for yourself is to die and who wants to do that? The issue is never how to manage time — it is always how to manage events in the time we have. Let me begin my presentation.

Mr Chairman, thank you for your kind welcome and your invitation to be here at your conference today. My key subject today is 'It's About Time'.

Time really is life and life is all we have. If ever there was a valuable concept it is this one. It's a way of creating urgency and focusing on priorities in our life. Along with goal-achieving, time is a critical factor in doing what needs to be done in order to achieve your goals, whatever they may be, because unless we use our time to achieve what is important to us we can become lost in the daily issues of life.

There is no such thing as time as we understand it with reference to clocks. They are man-made devices which make it possible for us to know what to do and when to do it. How to co-ordinate activity. How to be in the right place at the right time. How to catch the train, how to get to work and to get home again. The reality for every one of us is that life starts for each of us when we are born and finishes for us, according to our beliefs, when we die. Between being born and dying time flows endlessly. We can't manage time because time is a non-manageable resource, but we can manage events within the time we allot to them. We're going to get time whether we like it or not and at the same time and rate as every other person on earth. To realise that time really is life, just ask yourself what your chances are of getting younger. Of course, the answer will be none.

Time for each of us is simple: each day we get one day of our life and we take that day into the marketplace we call life and we trade it for whatever we are willing to take in return for the day we have just given away. How well we trade the days of our life depends on how much we value our life. Yet, without thinking, many give the days of their life away and in return get very little. What a tragedy. The only thing we have that is really beyond value we give away as if it is of little value. 'Time is at once the most valuable and the most perishable of all our possessions,' said writer Oliver Wendell Holmes. Time is not money, time is life. The value of understanding this concept is that it focuses our thinking on priorities that are important to us. If you believe that time equals money then stop work and find out how much money you make in the time you have when you are not working. Remember, a man or woman at work or a dollar at work are the only known ways of creating wealth. Your dollars may be earning but you won't be.

Procrastination is the enemy of many of us. We procrastinate about making the changes that are important in our life, we find it difficult to make up our mind and to turn our decision into a goal and focus our efforts on attaining that goal. Time really is life and life is all we have; for each day when we procrastinate about using that day in gaining our goals we are just using up more of our allotted time and getting little value for it. Remember, time is critical for all of us: yesterday is gone forever, tomorrow never comes, it's today, it's now, or it's never. Unhappily for many of us, time just goes by and we accomplish very little with it. We have sacrificed our chances on the altar of procrastination and what might have been has been lost to us.

But the point about procrastination is clear — it wastes time. Go for it, never give up the opportunity of deciding what you want in life. Make the decision, set the plan and go for it. It is not lack of opportunities that holds us back, it is the inability to overcome procrastination; fear of the possible losses that may occur for whatever reasons. Those fears hold us like prisoners and stop us from going after our dreams. Fears are imagined events put in the worst possible light. We need to see them in a better, more positive way. The clock is always ticking for each of us and there is no way of getting back the time that has gone, but we can make what we have left more urgent and achieve great things by never letting a day go by in which we have not made some progress towards what we most desire. Remember, time is life and life is all we have. Don't waste it. Build it into a glorious reminder of how you value it by your success.

Ten time-wasters and how to turn them into time-winners

Time-waster 1: lack of objectives, priorities and planning

This time-waster is likely to be evidenced in statements such as:

- If only I could do what I really wanted to do.
- If only I was in charge.
- Goals are not important; I tried setting them once or twice but it didn't work.
- Planning takes up too much time. I could have the work done while I am wasting time planning.
- I know priorities are important, but everything I do is top priority. I can't choose one ahead of the others because all of them have to be done.

Time-winner 1: lack of objectives, priorities and planning

The way to turn this time-waster into a time-winner is to become an effective planner. Control starts with planning, and self-control must exist within us before we can control what we do in our work and life. The events of life do not control us, we control them. The first act of being in charge is to plan. Planning and forecasting go together. Being good at forecasting makes planning much more effective.

Forecasting is looking into the future and, based on how you see today, deciding how the future might look when it arrives. The more accurate your observations, the better your chances. Then you set plans to take advantage of the opportunities you see, or to overcome the problems you believe will arise. Plans do not always succeed, but you rarely succeed by not planning.

Planning does take time and the more time and effort you put into it the more effective it is likely to be.

Start by accepting that the problem is not one of managing time, but one of managing events. The easiest way — the only way — to manage events is to identify worthwhile objectives, give them priorities and then plan how to achieve those objectives. Once your activities are focused on a day-to-day action plan designed to achieve your objectives, much of the problem will disappear.

Accept that discipline is a necessary part of being in charge and focus all your efforts on achieving your objective. Be kind to yourselves and reward yourselves each time you achieve a worthwhile goal. Life is to be enjoyed, not endured. Avoid becoming a workaholic. There are very few workaholics who are really successful. If we count the hours they work, their rate of pay is substantially lower than that of many other effective people. It doesn't take a genius to do twice the work in twice the time, it only takes someone who is willing to work twice as long. The real test of effectiveness is to achieve more in less time.

If lack of objectives, priorities and planning is one of your top 10 time-wasters you should immediately take action to overcome the problem by putting into effect the above suggestions.

Time-waster 2: crisis management

This time-waster is likely to be evidenced by statements such as:

- Not balance time again?
- Doesn't anyone but me do any work around here?
- How can I get my work done if someone always wants something else done?
- Sorry, I can't go to the meeting; I have to put out another fire.
- Life seems to be one crisis after another.
- Drop whatever you are doing and help with this.

Time-winner 2: crisis management

Are you involved in crisis management? Are you letting events run you? Have you not yet accepted that you're in charge of your thinking and that you have absolute control over your thoughts? Thoughts produce actions and actions based on sound objectives and priorities will take you out of the realms of crisis management. Actions will give you the opportunity to gain some useful time, destroy recurring problems and put you in charge of your life.

Crisis management is essentially a problem caused by waiting until the last minute, until something must be done before making any attempt to start it. Crisis management is a result of the failure to plan long term. Essentially, planning is resisted on the basis that it limits freedom of action. What we seem to forget in our day-to-day activity is that time is always limited while work never is. When we place emphasis on day-to-day operations and push planning for the future into the background, we are essentially putting out today's fires and creating the climate for crisis management. The misconception that the time taken to plan is wasted is paid for by crisis management, for which the cost is extremely high.

Almost everybody I know agrees with the importance of setting objectives, yet day-to-day activities seem to take priority over planning. In the long run the busy individual's only hope is to plan events in advance, to accept that they can be and are in charge of their own destiny — and that means planning in the future. Planning means commitment — and commitment to getting day-to-day plans done is the death of crisis management.

The first step you can take towards overcoming crisis management is to plan your time first, because it is limited, and then plan your work, which is rarely limited. Remember, work expands to fill the available time. When you know how much time you have, fill it up with the highest priority work you have. Realise that there will be work left over and delegate it to someone who has time to do it. Learn to say no to work you don't have time to do.

Much of what we do each day is repetitive, so in order to reduce the time spent on recurring problems we should turn them into procedures. Once these activities are systematised, much of the work is reduced to procedures that can often be delegated to someone else.

Crisis management can be seen at work, in the home, or at play. The solutions are the same no matter where the crisis is taking place.

Time-waster 3: telephone and email interruptions

The telephone and emails are the great communicators, or the great destroyers of personal effectiveness. Every day we hear comments like the following:

- The phone didn't stop ringing all day.
- Every time I went to do something the phone would ring.
- Am I the only person who answers the phone around here?
- Am I getting all the emails in this business?
- Why does everyone write to me?

Time-winner 3: telephone and email interruptions

All of these interruptions are self-inflicted. Nobody insists that we waste time by allowing telephones to interrupt what we are doing. (Service workers who rely on the phone are excluded from these comments; the phone had better keep ringing or there is no work!) If we run our lives and our work so that the telephone and the computer has the freedom to interrupt us whenever someone else chooses, there will be no solution to our problems.

The simple answer to telephone interruptions is to understand that we do have control over whether we take every call that comes in. We can choose how to handle the phone, whether it's at work, home, or play. Is the telephone the bane of your life? Do interruptions by telephone cost you dearly in terms of your time usage? If they do, the answer is simple. Make a rule that you are not available on the phone when you are actively working. Take no calls. Have calls intercepted by your secretary, or by someone else. Ask them to take messages if they are unable to deal with the situation themselves. At intervals, decided by you, go though all the calls that have been received, then set aside the time to answer the calls and solve the problems. You will be much more effective if you answer the calls at intervals of, say, one hour. If you must take a call, put a time limit on your answer. Try to finish each call in, say, three minutes. You will be surprised at how easily this can be done. Practice makes perfect, so keep on using this method until it becomes a habit. If you are going to be constantly available for telephone calls there is no answer to your problem.

If your work is done over the phone and you must always be available, use your time on the high-priority calls and make the rest as short as you can. The same problem exists with emails. They are an essential method of communication in business today but they must be systematised or they will drain your time away. Use the same technique as with the telephone: answer all emails that are of high priority on the hour, each hour, and in between time focus all your energies on your number one priority. Go through your emails and decide which ones you do not want to receive, especially those that are not directly connected with the important part of your work. If you are getting friendly time-waster emails be polite, but get in touch by email and ask that you be taken off their list unless the matter is directly involved with your work.

Time-waster 4: attempting too much

There is an element of 'I need to get involved in everything' about attempting too much; an 'I need to be seen to be busy' syndrome. The signs are nearly always the same:

- I have to do it to make sure it is done right.
- I am the only one who knows how.
- I don't have the time to train someone to do it.
- I know I should delegate but I don't have the time to set it up; it's easier to do it myself.
- Of course I can — just ask me any time you want.

Time-winner 4: attempting too much

Those who are the willing victims of this time-waster go to work early and they stay late. Their desks are piled high, their 'in' baskets are always full. At home or at play, it's the same: always busy, always willing to take on more. Activity is confused with contribution and effectiveness. The need to be seen to be busy is the critical issue for these people. They have not yet learned that time is limited but work rarely is. *There is no relationship between hard work, doing it all yourselves and positive accomplishment.* Almost everyone accepts the adage that we need to work smarter, not harder. Almost everyone who voices this view is in fact saying that hard work does not in itself guarantee accomplishment. Imagine for a moment what the manager to whom you report thinks about your work future when they see you constantly in a state of confusion.

Are you attempting too much? Are you spending your time on the futile exercise of always attempting more work than there is time available to accomplish it? If you are, you need to identify the really important priorities by asking yourselves these questions:

- What is my job?
- What contribution can I make to this organisation, that if I do not make it, will be left undone?
- How can I make my boss and my co-workers productive?
- What are my three most important objectives?
- Which are my top priorities and how best can I spend my time achieving them?

You need to accept that if time is limited but work never is, then some work will remain undone. You also need to accept that if the work that remains undone is high-priority work and if this high-priority work is the real contribution that you should be making to your organisation, then leaving it undone is going to harm your career. Accept also that much of what you do day to day could be left undone and it would never be noticed. The most effective solutions are to set priorities and objectives and to plan. Do what effective people do: plan your time first, which is limited, then fill up the available time with the highest priority work you have. That is a sure-fire way to overcome this time-waster.

Time-waster 5: personal disorganisation

- Are you a victim of personal disorganisation?
- Are you suffering from lack of objectives and priorities?
- Is crisis management ruling your life?

- Are telephone interruptions eating away your free time?
- Is attempting too much placing a giant load on you?
- Are ineffective delegation and procrastination causing you problems?

If they are, you must act now to overcome the problem, for there is no place at the top for disorganised people. Remember, if it is happening to you, then you will be making it happen to others.

Time-winner 5: personal disorganisation

The personal disorganisation time-waster seems to be the combination of any number of other time-wasters. It is the outcome of a lack of planning, the result of not understanding that before control can exist in a work situation, there must be self-control. Before management can exist in any situation, there must be self-management. It is the failure to plan on a day-to-day and long-range basis that makes personal disorganisation a major problem for a great number of people.

If disorganisation is a problem for you, the most positive action you can take is to become completely objective-oriented. Disregard all the irrelevant activities that go on around you and focus your entire time on the important things that you must get done. Work within the limits of your time, start each day 30 minutes early and in the quiet time of this early start, write your activity plan for the day and stick to it. Get in touch with those who depend on what you do and ask them how you can make what you do for them more effective to them — and do it.

There is no easy solution to personal disorganisation. The key issue is whether personal disorganisation is going to limit your contribution and your life, or whether you accept that you have a personal disorganisation problem and you do something about it so that it doesn't interfere with doing the high-priority work which is most likely to increase your chances of success.

There is no peace and very little pleasure for disorganised people, whether it is at work, at home, or at play. Quality of life is a critical issue for each of us. Life is meant to be enjoyed, not endured. We get one chance, one life to live, no repeat performance. It's now or it's never. Give yourselves every chance of enjoying every minute by substituting order and consistency in your life for chaos and confusion. The world in which we live is a beautiful place, full of pleasure and plenty, and it is here for each of us to enjoy if we will only take the time and make the effort.

Time-waster 6: drop-in visitors

This is the companion to telephone interruptions. It causes endless problems, wastes hours of valuable time and because many drop-in visits are of a social nature, they contribute very little to your productivity or your future.

- Are you running an open-door policy that encourages drop-in visitors?
- Is your workplace seen by others as a great place to have a break from work?
- Are you a ready and receptive listener?
- Do visitors provide you with welcome relief from the chores of your work?

- Do you often get behind, or accomplish less than you should, because you are too generous in allowing visitors to squander your time?
- Are you reluctant to discourage drop-in visitors because you may hurt their feelings, or because you fear you will be seen as abrupt or unfriendly?

Time-winner 6: drop-in visitors

If this sounds like you, but you want to make a change to avoid losing valuable time, then you need to start by closing the open door. Have all visitors screened and meet only those for whom you have set aside time. If you must meet with someone who has called without an appointment, stand up when they enter and stay standing until they leave. If you stand they won't sit. Once you stand, they won't stay long unless you encourage them. If you have to meet with someone, whenever possible go to their place as it is easier for you to leave them than to get them to leave you. Don't have spare chairs in your workplace because it literally asks drop-in visitors to move in. If they do come in, ask 'Can this be resolved in five minutes? I have to have this work finished and I am working against the clock.' Or say, 'I am sorry I can't talk now; I will give you a call in an hour' and when you call, restrict your call to three minutes. Never offer coffee unless it is important and you want to talk. If you work in an open office environment you need to work with your back towards the doorway and if possible place a sign on your outside wall that says 'busy' and underneath it 'not to be disturbed' and underneath that 'enter at your own risk' and place a tick against the message you want to give to those who are dropping in. This last statement will give you plenty of room to make their stay a short one. Once the word gets around that you are almost always too busy to socialise, much of your problem will disappear and if you apply this time to top-priority work your contribution and effectiveness will increase significantly.

Time-waster 7: lack of delegation

Whether you are running your household or a small or large business, the principles are the same. Time is limited, but work rarely is. In order to have more time to yourselves you need to spread the load to others. To test your need to improve your delegating skills, do a review of how often you delegate to subordinates. Those who are doing it all themselves should ask themselves these questions:

- Are you trying to do it all yourself?
- Do you feel that it is your duty, or is it that you think no one else can do it as well?
- Are you forever running out of time?
- Is the pressure getting to you?
- Are you working late?
- Are you afraid to let others make decisions?

Time-winner 7: lack of delegation

The above statements are the hallmarks of people who do not understand the nature of their problem. They can be seen in a frenzy of activity trying to catch up with work they have not been able to get done in the available time. It would seem logical to simply delegate some of the work to someone else.

It does not take a genius to do more work in 15 hours than a fellow worker does in eight. It simply takes someone who is willing to work that much longer. The sure test of effectiveness is the person who can work for the same length of time as everyone else and get twice as much done. That is increased productivity. Decide what part of your work could be done by someone else. Become a delegator. You are in for a pleasant surprise. Suddenly you have more time at your disposal. In life, there are many individuals who do not understand that effective home-makers, executives, managers and salespeople are forever trying to find someone else to do what they want done.

Delegating is not assigning. You assign a job to a worker, but you delegate responsibility to one of your co-workers. The difference between the two is largely that when you assign a job you are then responsible for both the person and the job. When you delegate you enlist the services of someone who can do the whole job independently and adequately.

The right time to delegate is whenever you can. Delegate when your workload is too heavy. Delegate before you go away on trips or holidays, and you will find that when you return the organisation seems to have done better while you were away. The world didn't end, nothing really bad happened. All that you proved is that life can go on without you and that is something we constantly need to remind ourselves of.

Delegate to the right people. Screen your people carefully. Study them at work, test them with problems, encourage their independent thinking, and don't expect perfection. Expect the best but remember that none of us is perfect. Select those with initiative and back them up when they take the initiative. Finally, keep track of the delegations you make, show interest in those you select and make time to go through their plans with them. Delegate the routine but stay in charge of the big picture.

Time-waster 8: indecision and procrastination

Individuals with this problem tend to express it in words like this:

- I will call you in a few days; I need to think about it.
- I know I said today, but something has come up. I will get to it as soon as I can.
- How long do I have to make up my mind?
- I need to consider other options.

Procrastination is the great time-waster and a great performance leveller. It is a habit for many people. The basic problem is that most indecisive people let lower-priority work take precedence over more important issues. Most tend to take the easy way out; they do what is easiest and at hand rather than thinking through and occupying themselves with higher-priority work. They complain of constant interruptions by others, yet psychologically they tend to welcome them because those interruptions fulfil their purpose, which is to fritter away their time by using it on low-priority work.

Time-winner 8: indecision and procrastination

Most of our procrastination problems are self-inflicted and could easily be eliminated if we had the willpower and the desire to do what needs to be done. Recognising and acting against procrastination is a constant need. There is no easy way to overcome procrastination; we have to be willing to undertake the discipline of assigning to ourselves only those things that are important to achieving our overall high-priority goals. Unless we are willing to become completely objective and priority-oriented, we are likely to fall victim to procrastination.

If you want to dramatically improve your effectiveness, identify those things you least like doing and do them extraordinarily well. When you do this, you will find that you have almost completely overcome procrastination, because once you tackle the things you least like doing there is no need to procrastinate.

Assigning priorities can sometimes cause procrastination because many of us react against and try to avoid the discipline that comes with the acceptance of priorities. A classic symptom of this is the statement, *Every goal I have is a top priority.* That may very well be true but you can only work on one thing at a time. Procrastination happens when no work is done because the decision on what is to be done cannot be made. Action is the death of procrastination so try to develop a method of decision-making that will result in action now. If you find yourselves procrastinating, ask yourself this question: 'Can I do anything to solve the problem?' If the answer is no, then forget the issue and cease procrastinating. If the answer is yes, then clarify what it is you can do and do it immediately. This may be difficult at first, but if you continue to use this simple method to initiate action, you will soon find it becomes second nature. Your effectiveness will increase and procrastination will cease to be a problem.

Time-waster 9: inability to say no

Most of us like to feel wanted. We would rather help than hinder. Many of us even say yes when we know there is little hope of actually doing what we have been asked to do.

- Do you find it difficult to say no?
- Do you need to accept that you can never do everything that everybody wants — there just isn't time?
- Are you wasting your time and your talents on a variety of activities?
- Is the inability to say 'no' one of your problems?
- Are you trying to please everyone by trying to meet every demand?
- Have you not yet realised that it's important for you not to let others fritter away your time and life?

Time-winner 9: inability to say no

In order to remove this time-waster, you have to be decisive. The best solution in most cases is to say no at the outset. If you use 'no' properly and with courtesy you can save a great deal of time without imposing any penalties on yourselves or those you deal with. It is rarely the 'no' that offends, it is nearly always the way it is said. There are few people who like rejection, so any time you say no, you should take care to explain the reason. Give your reason or reasons in detail and most people will understand.

Say no when you don't have to attend meetings. Say no when you don't need to travel. Say no to making appointments that others can manage for you. Say no to committees that won't achieve your objectives. Say no to work that will place an additional burden on you. Say no to becoming secretary, treasurer, or president of your club, unless it is one of your important goals and you have rearranged your affairs so you can do justice to the position and still lead a happy and productive life. Say, 'No, I can't do it now, but I can do it tomorrow.' Say no to your boss. Say, 'I do not have the time to do what you want now and complete the important work I am currently doing. However, if you prefer that I leave this and do what you have asked, that is all right with me, as long as you understand that what I am now doing will have to wait.'

Saying no rarely causes a problem. Saying yes, when it should have been no, is generally what causes the problem. Take charge of your life, decide your goals, prioritise them, set aside the time to get them done and don't get involved in anything that will lessen your chances of achieving them.

Time-waster 10: lack of self-discipline

This is all 10 time-wasters rolled into one. Without self-discipline you can be lost in the ebb and flow of life's demands.

- Is every day an exercise in you trying to do the impossible, or nothing at all?
- Are you placing yourselves at the mercy of events?
- Do you lack the self-discipline to get to the top?
- Do you not understand that to be in charge, you must first be in charge of yourselves?

Time-winner 10: lack of self-discipline

If lack of self-discipline is one of your problems give it all your attention and try to eradicate it from your life. You can do this by focusing all your time and energy on high-priority goals. Work in itself is not achievement. In the end we are paid for productivity, for reaching our potential, for doing those things that need to be done at the time. Self-discipline means that you do this every day, no matter what. Again you must ask yourself if this lack of self-discipline will limit your possibilities and your life. If you take the most important action that must be taken, no matter what the situation and despite everything else — despite all other interruptions, time-wasters and problems — and you manage to achieve those high-priority objectives which will give you the greatest chance of progress within your life and your career, congratulations. Self-discipline is ensuring that you do what needs to be done, no matter what other diversions arise. What is needed is the discipline to plan, to create priorities and to give each priority a value in terms of its importance to you and your organisation and then find the courage to see each one through to the end.

If you focus on the big picture and everything you want to accomplish, then it is likely that the size of the task will overwhelm you. It may be more useful to focus on one day at a time until you get into the habit of self-discipline. It takes around 21 days of continuous usage to build a new habit, so if for each of those 21 days you focus on exercising total discipline for that day, at the end of 21 days you will have established discipline in your life. For each day you win the battle, the next day will be a little easier, and each day is a victory which increases your motivation to continue. At the end of the time reward yourselves with something special: you will have earned it.

Let's recap

All time-wasters that we have dealt with fall within the ambit of our own authority. They are largely self-imposed, so if we solve time-waster number one — lack of objectives, priorities and plans — we will, to a large extent, solve most of our problems, because no matter what happens to us, our one overriding consideration at all times must be to achieve productivity and do those things that are important. We can be entirely free of time-wasters and still not achieve our goals. We can be belaboured by time-wasters and still achieve our goals and reach our potential if we make sure that the time we have spent is on high-priority work. The time to start is now: don't wait until you are perfect at using time. Perfection is rarely a possibility or a necessity. Remember, the real issue is not to save time, it is to achieve your goals, whether business or private. In order to win in life it is necessary to focus on contribution and effectiveness, not process and efficiency. You may be the most efficient performer of this decade, but if you are not focusing on contribution and identifying the major task you should be achieving, your efforts might count for little. Answering the mail the same day it arrives may be efficient but if it goes to the wrong person or doesn't answer the writer's questions, nothing is achieved. Using time effectively is a sure sign that we accept we are getting the same amount of time as every other person on earth and what we do with it decides the winners and losers in life.

There is no substitute for time. You are currently getting all there is — the same amount as every other person on earth. In any one day we each get 24 hours; you can't stretch them, you can't get more time, and the only way you can get less time is to die. Remember: geniuses get the same amount of time as mental incompetents. Millionaires get the same as paupers. Young the same as old. Workers the same as loafers. Teetotallers the same as drunks. Contribution by way of effectiveness is the key issue.

Now it is up to you. It's your life and it is you who must decide if you want to make changes that can bring you unlimited success. Only you know whether you will do what needs to be done. Time and thought are life and life is all we have. Time decides its duration and thought its quality. In life, we either win or lose; there are no draws. No time off, no replays, it's the grand final now and every day. The clock is always running. It's you and me in the game of life from the day we are born till the day we die. One chance and it's gone and we won't come this way again. One life to live in the glorious now. Don't waste a moment.

Remember, you can't waste time — you can only waste your life. Time is life and life is all you have. Like all other aspects of your life during this time of great change, innovation is the key to a better future. It doesn't happen by accident, it happens when you take charge of your life. Stop depending on out-of-date solutions to your problems and embrace innovation as the way to the future.

Thank you for listening. May your future be filled with success.

10. Goal-achieving – How to Win in Life

I have given this presentation at least 50 times to organisations of different types and sizes whose aspirations were often radically different, but always important. Goal-achieving is critical to all humans because it makes us focus on what is most important in our lives. A goal is a description of what we want in life. Of who we want to become. This presentation is featured in all my books because of its importance. I believe that the system contained in this presentation is the most effective method of goal-achieving available in the world today. It has been responsible for much of the success I have achieved in my career in business and in life. The only way the system can fail is if the individual using it does not follow the system exactly as it has been designed to work. There are no short cuts if you want to be sure to achieve your goal. Let me begin my presentation.

Mr Chairman, thank you for your kind welcome and for inviting me to make this presentation at your conference. The key subject today is 'Goal-achieving — How to Win in Life'.

We all need reminding at times that mental stagnation could happen to us if we become too complacent. There is no greater truth in today's world than the phrase, innovate or die. The easy days are gone. The first step in preparing your strategy for the future should be to formulate a goal. That goal could be any that is important to the organisation, or to you as an individual. For this presentation we will assume that you want to become successful in this new and different world that we will have to live and work in for the future. Becoming financially independent is another goal to challenge us. By that I mean achieving sufficient financial resources when you finish your working years to be able to support yourselves and anyone dependent on you, without having to lower your standard of living. The drive to achieve goals is a want which we can foster, and foster it we must if we are to succeed in achieving our goals, whatever they are.

Setting goals is not only a way to accomplish your possible dream, it is a basic human need. If we want to fill our lives with purpose and accomplishment, we need to set worthwhile goals that are important to us. The good news is that goal-achieving really works, because each of us is endowed with a brain that operates like a mechanical goal-seeking device; this quality separates humans from all other known life in the universe. It gives each of us the power to make judgements, consider options and to choose alternatives. It makes our dreams possible. Above all, it sets us free, fills us with hope and sustains us with a belief that empowers us to act according to our goals until they become a reality in our lives.

This marvellous goal-seeking mechanism within us operates automatically to achieve our goals for us. It is like a homing device on a guided missile. Once a missile is fired, the device is up and running, seeking the chosen target. If it gets off target it automatically corrects itself. It is locked onto the target. So it is with goal-setting; once we set the goal and start the activity necessary to achieve it, our mind computer and goal-seeking device is up and running. The mind's goal-seeking mechanism automatically operates to achieve the goal. All we have to do is keep it on target, which means we need to constantly check our progress towards our goal and when necessary, change and correct our course. If we constantly focus on the goal, the mechanism will ensure we hit the target.

We use this remarkable ability to set up failure or success. There is no middle ground. You will either get your goal, or you won't. The result of your failure to achieve your goal may be much better than the result if you had not attempted the goal. For example, you may get 50 per cent of what you had planned to achieve. So always remember that when you fail to plan, you automatically set up failure. Keep your goal constantly in your mind, focus all your energy on it. Your mind will do the rest.

When setting your goals the following four steps are a good starting point.

1. Set goals that are important to you, that will enrich your life and cause you to grow as a person as a result of having accomplished them.
2. List the daily actions that will, if implemented, achieve your goals. (Because of the importance of these daily action plans we will deal with them as a separate issue.)
3. List the attitudes that will help you take these actions, so they will become a reality in your life.
4. Train yourselves to absorb these actions and attitudes into your nervous system until they become automatic.

You will achieve what you focus on *because it is an unalterable law of life that what you think and believe is what you get.* So constantly hold in your mind the image of what you want to achieve. The more vividly you can imagine the result you want, the more certain it is that you will achieve it. Remember that emotion is the messenger that takes your desire to the subconscious mind. The more vividly you see what you want, the more certain it is that it will become yours. When setting your goals focus on the results, not the process: this is a critical factor for those who want to win. This doesn't mean that getting goals should be unpleasant and difficult. What it means is that life seems to demand of us more than a pleasant or easy existence. It is said that losers in life will do anything to achieve a pleasing method, or process, while winners will endure any pain to get a pleasing result. *This is the issue that separates winners from losers.*

Pay little and you get little from life; want little from life and the price is small. The more you want, the more it costs. Success is limited by the price we are willing to pay. The price is not only paid in money. It is paid in knowledge, activity, creative thinking, *innovation*, identification, preparation, commitment and compromise. So be prepared to embrace all these issues in your efforts to win your goal.

Compromise on your part will be necessary. All life is a compromise. Trading off one aspiration against another will always be necessary, for it indicates your willingness to pay whatever price is necessary to achieve your goals. Above all, you have to decide what you have to give in return for what it is you want to achieve. Everything in life costs. Sometimes the price is small, sometimes it is very high, yet small or high, it is the price and the constant demand made on you that will call into question your willingness to pay the price and win. Clearly define your goal, prepare yourselves for the journey, then commit yourselves to the job ahead. Recognise that it won't be easy, and everything has a price. But if you're willing to pay the price and commit yourself to the attainment of your goal you are almost certain to get it.

Setting your goals

Start with your lifetime goals, with whatever goal is most important to you. In the following example, the most important goal for you is to achieve financial independence. You will have other goals and the principles outlined here will not only help you to get your major goal of financial independence, but also any other goal that is important to you.

Writing valid goals

For a goal to be valid it must contain the following four elements:

1. It must be specific.
2. It must be time-bounded.
3. It must be measurable.
4. It must be achievable.

If any of these is missing you're largely wasting your time. If your goal is not specific you will have no focus, no target to aim for. Your goal-seeking mechanism will be unable to start because it has no specific instructions.

Assume for the purposes of this illustration that you are 35 years of age and you plan to cease working at age 60. Now write your goal in output terms so that you will achieve a possible positive result. Your goal could read like this: *By my sixtieth birthday I will have achieved my goal of financial independence by amassing tangible assets to the value of $1 million in today's values.* Substitute your goal for my example. You should now identify a measurement method so that you will know when you have achieved your goal. The measurement method could be: *The $1 million of net assets will be in my bank account, in real estate, (including my home) in shares, or other investment types that are readily negotiable.*

Getting your goals

Achieving your goals is the key to your happiness and success. Humans are goal-seeking by nature. Without goals they have little purpose in life, they lack the direction that goals provide. This lack of purpose and direction is made manifest by a loss of motivation on the part of individuals, which results in their failing to reach their potential in life. If we are not living to get our lifetime goals, what are we here for? What else is there?

Your major objective is to get the goal; so far all you have done is set the goal. Almost anyone can do that part. It's getting the goal that shortens the list of those who succeed.

Remember to take account of, and never forget, that work in itself is not accomplishment. If it were, those who worked hardest would always win, but you know that is not true. If hard work in itself was the answer then goals would be easy to achieve. If you think that hard work is the answer, do this exercise. First, think of a person, or persons who have, in your opinion, been outstandingly successful in their life. They didn't win it, or inherit it, or if they did they increased it through their own efforts. Now ask yourself: did they work hard to achieve their success? The answer in most cases will be yes. Now ask yourself: how many people do you know who have been working their tails off for years and getting nowhere? You will probably know hundreds — and the hundreds may include yourselves.

The paradox of work is simple: if you think you can be outstandingly successful without working hard you will be bitterly disappointed. If you think that hard work by itself will make you successful you will be equally disappointed, because success requires imagination, creativity and innovation applied to real-life goals in a purposeful way. It requires faith and belief in ourselves and in our goals, belief that they have been worthwhile in every sense. Do not be put off, or inhibited by the words 'imagination' and 'creativity'. You have all that is needed to achieve your most important goal of achieving financial independence by age 60.

Getting goals is not always easy. If it were, everyone would be rich, happy and contented. To achieve your goal perspiration is necessary; hard work is always on the side of those who want to win. But inspiration is also essential. It is said that a drop of inspiration is worth a bucket of perspiration, so simply identifying and listing goals in priority order will not accomplish your end. Something more is required: that something is the creative twist to what you're going to do. Creative goals are the answer. Goals that are worth working for, goals that test and improve your abilities, goals that strengthen your character, goals that build a better life for yourselves and those you love and care for. Goals that will be big enough to ensure you grow as a person as a result of achieving them.

Ten ways to help you get your goals

As we go through the 10 ways listed below, check each one to ensure you are taking account of it in your planning.

1. Balance your picture

Do your goals fit your total picture? Are they in harmony with your current lifestyle? If not, are you willing to alter your life? Are your goals consistent with your aspirations? Are you heading in the same direction as your partner in life? Are your goals a balanced view of life from others' perspective? If they are not, it will make them more difficult to achieve — not impossible, just more difficult. Remember that goals should be tools to get what you want, they should not be seen as your master. You are in charge of what you want; your goals are only the way to go about getting what you want.

2. Align your goals

Try to ensure that as you work on goal one you're making a contribution to goal two. As you work on goal two, make a contribution to goal three. This is how consistency can save you time and effort. Never stop focusing on what it is that you want to achieve. Make sure that every activity you undertake is making a contribution to all of your goals.

3. Co-operate

Most people from whom you want help will be glad to give it, sometimes even at the expense of their own goals. But you need to ask for their help. They are not mind-readers. You can pay no greater compliment than to say, 'I have a goal that is important to me and I believe you can help me. Would you do this for me please? I will be happy to return the favour by helping you achieve your goal. Is that fair enough?'

4. Visualise what you want, not what you want to avoid

At all times focus on what you want until it becomes your dominant thought. Dominant thinking is a law of life. Humans cannot move away from what they do not want, they can only move towards what they do want. Traditional goal-achieving methods and systems did not take into account the power of our minds and the role that visualisation plays in goal-achieving. As a result, those methods constantly failed to achieve the goals that were set.

5. Have a clear image of what you want

Quantify it, time bound it, make sure it is measurable. Make sure it is attainable. For without a clear image of what you want, you cannot visualise it on the life screen of your mind. If you can't see it, you can't do it. It's impossible for you to accomplish anything without first visualising what it is you want to achieve. This is a law of life, necessary to all achievement: nothing can be done until it is first seen in our imagination. First create the picture in your mind; with it all things are possible, without the picture nothing creative is possible.

As an example, I am going to ask you to do something and I want you to think closely about what you did mentally before you physically did what I asked. You are at home. Here is the instruction. *I want you to get the mail from your letterbox.*

Now think of what happened before you could get the mail. Here is what happened. As soon as you heard the question you immediately saw your letterbox as a picture in your mind. You saw yourselves taking the mail out of your letterbox and bringing it inside your home so that you could show that you had carried out the instruction. If you had not visualised your letterbox you could not have done that. First the thought, then the picture, then the action. That is why it is so important for you to continually see in your imagination your goal. The more brightly it burns in your mind the more certain it is that you will achieve your goal.

6. Accept responsibility

Once you accept absolute responsibility for the actions you take in order to get your goals, you will look at life differently. Actions take on a new meaning, options look more real, possibilities unfold that previously you didn't see. This is the power of self-determination at work in your life. Many people choose to ignore or deny their right to self-determination but that doesn't mean it doesn't exist. It simply means they exercise their right not to act. For reasons known only to themselves, through their disbelief they deny themselves all the benefits by not accepting what comes their way. It really is a sad choice.

7. Set a time frame for accomplishment

Nothing generates action more effectively than setting a date by which time a goal will be accomplished. Be specific. (By my sixtieth birthday I will have achieved my goal of financial independence by amassing tangible assets to the value of $1 million in today's values.) Depending on how much or how little time you have before your expected retirement you may wish to increase or decrease your monetary goal. My choice of $1 million and age 60 are only for illustration purposes.

Because the goal is so far into the future you may decide to start taking action in the future instead of today. If you decide to do that, you are already on the road to failure. That is why the goal system requires you to set a plan that will start today and then it will require you to constantly update the activities you must do and the mini-goals you must achieve in order to accomplish your major goal of achieving financial independence. Remember, it is always possible that you will achieve your goal by the time you are 50, or even earlier, but planning will ensure you achieve it at 60. If it should happen that you reach your goal by age 50, then increase your goal to $2 million because at that time you have a million dollars of assets on which to build your next millions. There is no end to the possibilities of wealth creation once you have started on your journey. Every day will bring new ideas about how you can continue to grow your wealth. Foster the 'everything is possible' attitude and go for what you want.

8. Know when you have achieved your goal

It's important to clearly define how you will know you have successfully achieved your goal. This means you have to measure what is done. Work must be measured if for no other reason than to measure your progress. Your measurement method could be, 'The $1 million of net assets will be in my bank account, in real estate (including my home), in shares, or other investment types that are readily negotiable'. In order to be sure you are not getting behind target you need to constantly measure your progress. Do not become disillusioned if your investments appear to have stalled, or even go backwards for a short time. Your plan is a long-term goal and investments do not always grow in a consistent manner, but over the long term they will grow.

9. Check on progress

Set dates of review, constantly check how you're going, whether you're on time, on target. If not why not and how do you plan to get back on target again? Few of us would ever commence holidays without a destination and a time of planned arrival, yet many of us journey through life without such a plan. Knowing your destination is important to your every success. For example, when a captain of a ship is leaving the port, he must plan his course, decide his next port of call and tell someone else of his destination and estimated arrival time. *Remember, when a ship misses the harbour there is no recorded instance of it being the fault of the harbour.* There is a lesson in this. The purpose of constantly checking against planned progress is to make sure that if we depart from our plan we know about it as soon as possible. Finding out too late may mean no possibility of recovery. At best it will mean a lot of unnecessary work.

10. Write down the how-to of your plan

Put your goals down in writing. That's the key to your success. Then prepare a separate detailed activity plan to achieve each of your goals — that's the whole secret; write your activity plan in detail. Most methods of goal-achieving finish at defining what it is they want. *The real issue is not what we want, the real issue is how to get what we want* and that's what you should now deal with by writing down in output terms all the activities you will need to undertake in order to achieve your goal of financial independence.

When questioning why you should write your plans down and in particular the activity that you need to undertake to achieve your plan, ask yourself this question: how long is it since I have taken an hour, two hours, more especially a whole day, or a whole week to sit down and really go through this planning operation as if my life really counted? Sadly, in too many cases the answer will be that you have never ever done it in this much detail. Does that mean you cannot succeed without doing it? No, it doesn't: there is more than one road to Rome. There is more than one way to do things. This is not the only way, but if you want to win more often, to win more, to do it more easily, more quickly, be more in charge, have fewer problems, then plan what it is that you want to do, write it down and then do it.

Here is an example of why this method is so effective. Some years ago a small survey was carried out in the

United States on the productivity of 30 people. All of the 30 people were highly successful by American standards; multi-millionaires and first-class achievers. Each of them was asked two questions. The first question was, 'Do you write down your plans?' Twenty-four said 'No', six said 'Yes'. Which seems to say that you do not have to write your goals down to be successful. The researcher then asked the second question, which was, 'What have you achieved so far in your life?' Then they checked the total productivity of the 30 people. They discovered that the 24 who did not write down their plans had achieved 40 per cent of the group's total achievement and the six who had written their plans down had achieved the other 60 per cent of the total. Which seems to say that writing down the how-to of your plans will enable you to be more effective than doing it in your head.

Another research project was undertaken recently which showed that of 100 per cent of people reaching retirement, less than 15 per cent had reached financial independence. *The researchers went on to say that in trying to identify the traits which separated the successful from the not so successful, the only consistent pattern they found was that those who had achieved financial independence had almost always written down their plans.*

If you want to be a champion at managing your life and getting your goals, if you want to do it smarter and not harder, if you want to work less and have more time for yourself and your family, if you want to get more and get it quicker, if you want to do more, if you want to be more, then write your plans down. You can do this by writing down the how-to of what it is that you want to get done.

How to write your goal

Now it's time to tackle the payoff section, the how-to of getting your goal. To complete this, focus on the example goal of becoming financially independent by age 60, or whatever age you want. Now you are making real progress. You have your goal written down. You have written down a plan to measure the attainment of your goal. You now have a list of activities designed to successfully achieve your goal. Now do the following:

a) Write your goal in the goal section of your goal record sheet. Use the example below as a guide.

b) In the section marked 'Measurement method' write how you propose to measure the successful attainment of your goal.

c) Plan the activities you need to carry out to achieve your goal. Think them through. This is the heart of the method. Stay with it until you know how to get your goal. If you can't decide what to do to get your goal, how are you going to get it? Remember, wanting to get a goal is easy. Getting it is more difficult. It requires much planning and decision-making. It requires creativity, but above all it requires a lot of common sense and an iron will to carry out your activity plan.

d) Now write your activities into your goal-getting sheet. Write them in sequential order under 'Plan to achieve objective', so that you are doing what needs to be done to get your goal in a logical, planned way. Include the name of the person who has responsibility for carrying out the activity, if this is applicable.

e) Number your activities from 1, placing the numeral in the column headed 'Item'.

f) Decide the date by which you will finish each activity. Write the date under the heading 'To be completed by'. Make sure each activity has a specific completion date.

g) As you complete each planned activity, sign it off in the column headed 'Date completed'. Sign it off by entering the date on which you completed the activity and initialling the date. This will be a constant check on whether you are completing your activities on time as planned.

h) The following section contains an example of how you should go about writing down your plan. Stick to the procedure, but write the specifics of your plan in the manner shown in the example.

i) You will no doubt have more than one goal, so you need a separate goal sheet for each goal. It is possible to have 10 or more goals. If you have more than one, give each goal a priority number in accordance to its importance in your total planning.

The following table includes only examples of how you could proceed. The final decisions about what you are prepared to do in order to achieve your goals are up to you. The number of items on your goal sheet will be decided by the number of activities needed to accomplish your goal. You may have to use more than one goal sheet to do what needs to be done. You may find that other people are able to help by doing some of the activities. If this happens, write them into your plan and give them the specific date you require them to finish the activity by. Do not let them hold up your plan.

In the example shown, Items 4–6 of the plan will require a mini-goal on a separate goal sheet. There may be other items, too, that you have in your completed plan that need

GOAL RECORD SHEET			
Goal: By / / I will have amassed assets over liabilities to an amount of $ .... in current money values.			Priority 1
Measurement method: Using information from my accountant showing my financial position in terms of assets over liabilities.			
Item	**Plan to Achieve Objective**	To be completed by	Date completed
1	Do an assessment of current financial position.		
2	Prepare a realistic budget of current expenses.		
3	Go through the budget and eliminate any expense that seems unnecessary. Do not eliminate all expenses for enjoyment. If the budget is too strict it will soon fall by the wayside.		
4	Cancel all credit cards except those that are absolutely necessary and which can be paid in full and avoid interest payments.		
5	If I do not own my own home, prepare a savings-and-investment plan that will enable me to have the deposit by / / . This is step 1 in creating wealth.		
6	Prepare a plan of self-development to improve earning power. This is step 2 in creating wealth.		
7	From my next income instalment and every future one, pay myself first the amount that I need to accomplish my goal of achieving financial independence.		
8	Deposit or invest that money the way I have decided in Item 5 above.		

to be written on a separate goal sheet. Number each separate goal sheet in the priority order you see them being done.

When you have accomplished the above planning and have your plans written down, you should do the following. Have someone whose judgement you trust look over your plan to identify difficulties or opportunities you may have overlooked. Check your timing; make sure you have left sufficient time to carry out the plans you have set in place. Make sure that if you require help from someone else they are willing to help and that they can do what needs to be done by the date you have in your plan. Do not let your plans stall because of someone else's inactivity. Always say, 'Can you do this for me by this date, because I cannot continue my plan until this part is accomplished. I appreciate your help and am willing to repay the compliment by helping you when required.'

The daily 'Must do today' list is a critical part of the whole goal-achieving plan. It requires that each day you decide what can be done to achieve progress in your plan to create wealth in your life. Write in your 'Must do today' list the things you must do — and do them. If you are self-employed this will not be difficult. If you are not then you will be restricted by what you can do to increase your effectiveness in your present employment. After business hours you can pursue other parts of your plan.

All that is required to make your list effective is for you to record your planned activities for the day as well as your appointments for the day. The planned activities are those that come from your goal sheets.

It is on record that a business consultant named Ivy Lee was hired by Charles Schwab, who at that time was the President of Bethlehem Steel, to advise him on the best ways to improve the effectiveness of the company. After doing his research Ivy Lee advised Charles Schwab that he should get all of his senior executives and the teams under their direction to use a simple 'Must do today' list and make sure they did what they planned. Some months later Charles Schwab told Ivy Lee that it was the most valuable advice he had received up to that point. He asked him how much he owed and Lee said, 'Pay what you think it was worth to you'. Charles Schwab paid Ivy Lee a considerable amount of money for the idea. Later on, Bethlehem Steel became the biggest producer of steel in the world.

Your plan will require constant attention and should be reviewed every day to make sure you are on track. If changes have to be made, make them and carry on. If you find you are continually making changes to your plan of action you need to pay more attention to getting the activities right in the first place. There is no substitute for getting things right the first time. It saves time and getting it right gives you that success feeling that develops good thinking habits.

This is not a chore you have to do against your will; this is your life and you will be the main beneficiary of the success of your plan. Don't put it off. Every day counts. For example, for your goal of achieving financial independence, the longer you have till the day you quit work, the more time for compound interest to work its magic in your life. The magic does not reside in the type of investment, it resides in compound interest. One important discipline we should observe at all times is to *think big* and go forward with confidence to make every day count. Every day you work on your plan, think of what Charles Darwin meant when he said, 'A man who dares to waste one hour of life has not discovered the value of life'. Now it is time to develop your strategy so that you can achieve this all-important goal.

The positive outcomes of implementing goal strategies in your life

By developing your strategy and then using the goal system illustrated in this chapter you will revolutionise your chances of success. You will be able to work on more goals at the one time because the structure makes that possible. You will be in full control all the time because the how-to of your plan has been written down. You can employ the skills of others to help you get your goal because the system holds them to their commitments. You will rarely if ever find another goal system as effective as this one.

This method will enhance your chances of self-improvement, make you more effective and increase your worth to your employer, or increase your profits if you are self-employed. It has been proven in many research projects that writing your goals down multiplies your chances of succeeding beyond the normal. This system will give you that advantage and make it possible for you to reach your goals sooner because you will be getting the benefit of a method that has been proven worldwide. So go for your goals with every talent you have. It's your life and only you can make it happen. Remember, there is no future in the past. Today it is innovate or die.

Thank you for listening. It has been my pleasure to be with you today and I wish you every success in your future activities.

11. When Your Customer Wins, You Can't Lose

I wrote a best-selling book on this subject and title. As a speaker/presenter I was constantly being asked to make presentations on the subject of customers to all kinds of businesses. The businesses wanted to know how they could increase their business and build their customer base. A majority of businesses know what should and could be done to win permanent customers, but they do not consistently do what they know. In this presentation on building customer loyalty I was presenting to a monthly Business MasterClass Seminar of business owners and managers. Business MasterClass Seminars is owned by one of my companies of the same name and is a seminar conducted by others under licence. Let me begin.

Mr Chairman, thank you for your kind welcome to this monthly Business MasterClass Seminar. My presentation is about creating and developing customers for your business.

The only real potential a business has is in its staff and customers and too often both are neglected by management. Products, services, location, knowledge and finance are all important, but limited and fairly short term in their potential. The potential of customers, however, is only limited by the imagination and innovation of a business's staff and the expectations of our customers and ourselves. If only we could remove the blinkers that prevent us from realising the enormous potential for growth and increased profits within the grasp of those who focus all their decisions, activities and energies on satisfying the customer. For those who can transform doing business to a simple enjoyable experience for their customers, the pay off will be exceptional. Let me emphasise that there are no clever and innovative businesses. There are only businesses that employ clever and innovative people. A business has no life in itself. It lives only through its people.

Simply because they have few options, customers suffer the frustration of having to do business with organisations that don't serve them well. The alternative of changing to some other supplier may not seem much better than the current situation, but what if there were a real alternative, one that would give enjoyment and satisfaction instead of anger and frustration? Or pleasure instead of pain? Today an emphasis on customer service is sweeping the world because it is seen as a key issue in business survival. This is happening because, important as conventional resources are, a business can no longer depend on them to guarantee long-term survival. As important as location is, a business can no longer depend on this to guarantee its long-term survival. Modern transport and communication provide almost unlimited access to all businesses. Special or unique products or services no longer guarantee long-term survival for a business either. Modern manufacturing and distribution methods and solutions mean that the competition is swift and tough, and that while choice may be limited today, it will be freely available tomorrow. Other resources, including finance, are generally so freely available that their advantages become strictly short term in the sense of providing a business with a means of survival.

While all of these factors are important to an enterprise, none will guarantee its success. Not having them may limit your chances, but having them is certainly no guarantee of success. All other issues being equal, only customer satisfaction will guarantee the long-term survival of a business in today's competitive markets.

Today competition is fierce, and it will grow even fiercer. Today nation competes with nation, state with state, city with city, town with town, and businesses at every level compete with other businesses. At every level of business activity, organisations are fighting for supremacy and survival. Business is not easy.

The limiting factor is always the customer. Today you may not have very much competition in your location. Tomorrow it may arrive in force.

Here is a key observation that you should make about your competitors. Firstly, your opposition in terms of products is a key competitor: once the prospective customer has made a decision to buy a product you sell, then you and your opposition are in competition and the customer will decide which business to buy from, using their own criteria. But before the prospective customer decides on the product you sell, they can spend their money on any one of a hundred different products or services. Your key marketing initiative at all times is to make your product or service appealing to all sections of the community, not just those who want the product you sell. Before a prospective customer decides on making a purchase they always weigh up their options. Unless you are in their initial decision-making calculations you have no hope.

If they are to survive and prosper over the longer term, businesses must decide that the customer really is 'king'. The purpose of business is to create customers. Customers create profits. Customers have little interest in the business, why it exists, who it exists for, who exists within the business, or who owns the business. Customers are driven by their wants and needs. If you have what they want at the right time and price they will usually do business with you. Whether or not they come back is a different matter.

Why customers quit

Why do customers quit? Why do they stop dealing with a particular business? Is there a pattern to why they quit? Research tells us that there is; it shows that the reasons customers give for leaving a particular business are remarkably consistent. Let us look at some statistics produced by this research.

Facts to make you think

Of all dissatisfied customers, 4 per cent are moved to complain; the other 96 per cent generally go quietly away, and 91 per cent will never come back. These are dissatisfied customers, not customers with a one-off complaint. Three per cent move away from the locality. Five per cent develop other friendships or relationships and they take their business where those friendships or relationships are. Nine per cent leave because of the competition. Maybe the prices are better, or the perceived value, or the service is better. So these customers move on to another business. But the key is that only nine out of 100 are leaving because of the competition. Think of the number of businesses that see price as the major reason for customers leaving. As a result of price-cutting, many businesses are needlessly taking lower margins. They slash prices, but customers still leave. Fourteen per cent are dissatisfied with the product. They go to another business where they believe a better product is available. How often do businesses research their customers to find out the level of satisfaction with the products and services that they sell? Sixty-eight per cent of customers said that they left because they were not valued. They left the business because of indifference shown to them by the business owner, manager, or employees. This is the crux of why customers quit.

What happens when customers leave

A typically dissatisfied customer tells eight to ten people of their dissatisfaction. One in five of those who are dissatisfied will tell 20 people about their dissatisfaction. In all, five dissatisfied customers will in total tell 60 people of their unhappy experiences. That's 60 people who have now been given an unfavourable view of your business, 60 people who are likely to repeat it many more times. Bad news travels fast, and good news rarely overtakes it.

What we can do to improve things

Seven out of ten complaining customers will do business with you again if you resolve the complaint in their favour. Ninety-five per cent will do business with you again if you resolve the complaint on the spot. The critical question to ask is: are your front-line staff members empowered to make decisions now, or must they seek approval from higher up? If they have to go to someone else for a decision, the odds are against their successfully solving the problem.

The answer is to empower the front-line staff. A satisfied 'complainer' will tell five people about the satisfactory outcome of the complaint, so the time you put in to resolving complaints to the customer's satisfaction will pay off handsomely. Now you can have customers out there where it counts, working on your behalf.

What it costs to win customers

It costs six times as much to attract a new customer as it does to keep an existing one. That's right, six times as much. On mathematics alone, it would seem wise for businesses to invest more money in keeping existing customers, rather than letting them leave because of lack of attention and then trying to replace them with new customers. Research gives us a simplistic but important general explanation for customers quitting. The overall reason that emerges is always the same. The people within the business don't pay enough attention to people problems. They appear to not value their customers.

Does that mean that anyone who buys from a particular business should never shop anywhere else? No, it doesn't. That would be an unrealistic expectation. Sometimes the business won't have what they want, and they will go somewhere else to buy it, but will they come back next time? That is the real issue. If we have built customer loyalty based on providing outstanding customer satisfaction, our customers will come back. If when we don't have what they want we tell them where they can get it and ensure they realise this is one of the rare occasions we don't have what they want, then they probably will come back.

Five ways to keep customers

1. Keep in touch with your customers and constantly let them know they are valued.
2. Turn customers on to your business. Make doing business with you a pleasure for the customer.
3. Make sure *all* your staff are turned on to customer service.
4. Resolve complaints quickly and in favour of the customer.
5. Do more than you promise and do it on time.

When the customer feels unappreciated

The solution is very simple. Treat every customer as if they are the most important customer of the business. Make every customer feel valued. Today's small buyer may easily become tomorrow's big spender. Every letter written to a customer should contain at least one statement that says, or implies, in easy-to-understand language, that the customer is valued by the business. The customer cannot read or hear this kind of message too often.

Here is an example. A friend of mine was recently shopping in a large department store. His wife had asked him to buy her a new electric iron. He was shown a number of irons ranging in price from $50 to $150. When he asked, 'What is the difference between the lowest and highest priced irons?' he was told $100. He tried again: 'Why should I pay the difference of $100?' He was told, 'Because you can afford it.' Being persistent, he tried again and at length, asking, 'What is the difference in the irons other than price?' The salesperson said, 'I don't know.'

The answer to this problem would seem to be that staff should bring themselves up to date on the products and services they sell on behalf of the business for which they work. If salespeople don't know the answer, they should let the customer know that they will find out and then get in touch with the customer and give them the information.

Five ways to avoid complaints

1. Train your staff in first-class telephone techniques and make sure your phone system is effective.
2. Answer all written complaints or queries promptly and effectively.
3. Insist that customers are dealt with quickly and effectively. Do not let staff socialise at the expense of customers.

4. Make regular checks to ensure your customer service standards are met.
5. Run regular training sessions to keep the skill level of your staff high.

Be customer-focused

Most businesses are run to suit the management or staff, not the customers. Many practices become part of a business not because they are aimed at making the customers' lives easier and more pleasant, but because they make life easier and more pleasant for those who work for the business. For example, we recently stayed overnight in a motel in an inland city of New South Wales. The motel was new and very pleasant, although not very soundproof. Far into the night and the early morning we listened to the TV set next door. Sleep was hard to come by. Later that morning, I was astounded to find that only six of the 40 rooms had been occupied. The six groups of guests had been accommodated in adjoining rooms. When booking out, I asked why the guests had been given adjoining rooms instead of having an unoccupied room between each occupied room. I was told the arrangement made it easier for the housemaids to clean the rooms. The guests were profit, the housemaids were cost, yet management focused its efforts on making the staff's work easier at the expense of making the guests' stay more pleasant. We will never stay at that motel again and I am sure we are not alone in making that decision.

Compare that situation to a recent experience while we were staying at another hotel in Melbourne. The weather had turned very cold, and we rang Housekeeping to see if it was possible to get a small heater. (Air-conditioning doesn't solve the problem when you are allergic to it.) The answer: 'No problem, I will send one up immediately.' The heater arrived, and was very effective. Thirty minutes later, a call came from the housekeeper: 'Are you warm enough? Would you like another heater? Is there anything else we can do to make your stay more comfortable?' Now that's more like service focused on the needs and wants of the customer and when we go back to Melbourne, guess where we will stay if possible.

How a business deals with moments of opportunity

A business's moments of choice can be described as moments of truth or moments of opportunity, but whatever the description, the issue is that the person acting on behalf of the business has at that precise moment a choice as to how they will respond to the customer's needs. A business is in contact with its customers every day and in many ways. Contact occurs every time a customer phones, makes contact face to face, or writes to the business. Every time the business responds, every time — at every level in an organisation — that an employee has to make a decision or carry out an action which is going to impact on customers, a moment of opportunity exists. Moments of opportunity are so critical because they decide the longer term fate of the business.

How a business rewards its staff for service to customers

Michael LeBoeuf, author of *The Greatest Management Principle in the World*, once said to me that the greatest principle is: 'What gets rewarded gets done.' I believe that this principle is beyond challenge. Everywhere in our lives, in both personal relationships and business relationships, it holds good. People do things if they know they will be rewarded for them, and the reason most businesses do not have an excellent customer satisfaction record is that excellent service is rarely rewarded at any level. Most businesses hire staff, give them very little training, give them even fewer examples to follow, and then expect them somehow to produce superior customer service.

Five ways to value customers

1. Make sure the focus of your staff is on the customer and not only on the process of running the business.
2. Run your entire business to suit the customer.
3. Make sure that 'moments of opportunity' are understood and implemented by every staff member, whether they directly serve customers or work behind the scenes.
4. Reward staff for excellent customer service.
5. Ensure that every person in your employ understands that it is the customer who pays their wages and salaries.

Creating customer satisfaction

The key to creating customer satisfaction is, firstly, to recognise that it is in the area of customer care and satisfaction that the real opportunities lie for increasing the amount of business we do, and the growth and success of our businesses, and for improving our careers within business. Secondly, we should recognise that superior customer care and satisfaction is achieved by doing a combination of hundreds of little things very well, rather than by doing several big things extraordinarily well. Thirdly, we should accept that the purpose of business is to create customers, and that customers are a necessity: your business is your customer.

Customers are not always easy to deal with

They are often self-centred and arrogant, and at times they can be rude and ungrateful. They tend to take what we do well for granted, no matter how big or important it is. Things we do badly or the least effectively, no matter how small they are, are held against us. For example, you may have had something new built or installed in your home. Those doing the job did the installation exceptionally well, but failed to clean up afterwards. Did you remember the exceptional job, or the fact that they made a mess which they did not clean up?

What is done well is never compared proportionally to what is not done well.

There are no earth-shaking decisions to be made that, if taken, will transform a business in the area of customer care.

It simply requires a hard slog at every level of the organisation to make sure that the hundreds of opportunities we get each day to serve our customers well are acted upon and turned into positive experiences for the customer and therefore pluses for us.

Here is an important question that businesses should ask of their organisation. How often does the owner or manager of a business ask for and get a complete report on 'Customer Care'?

Dealing with customers

Customers are driven by their wants and needs. They buy for only two reasons: to solve a problem, or to make themselves feel good. Creating customer satisfaction is always about relationships, which means how the customers feel about themselves, about you, about the business itself and about the product or service they require. Relationships are always the critical issue, and they are decided by the behaviour of the customer and the person in contact with them at the time the customer is seeking to make themself feel good or solve a problem. Any behaviour is an extension of one of four states of emotion: being glad, sad, mad or afraid. Both customers and the staff of the business will always be in one of these states — happy or fearful, sad, or angry and full of hatred. Imagine the consequences of both customer and staff member being angry at the one time. It would seem that the most desirable state for both parties would be to be glad; a feeling of well-being which would most likely draw good, receptive responses from both parties and result in a friendly, positive climate in which a mutually beneficial relationship could exist. Every customer has the right to expect good service, civil conduct and good manners from employees of a business with which they are dealing. The employee has a responsibility to the employer to accept this situation.

Five ways to satisfy customers

1. Give prompt, efficient and pleasant service to every customer.
2. Pay attention to each customer so they feel they are special.
3. Use their name as often as reasonably possible.
4. Remember, customers are not always happy or pleasant, so work hard to make them feel valued.
5. Go the extra mile to give outstanding service and satisfaction. Thank the customer for doing business with you and ask them to come back again.

How to use moments of opportunity

You should do the following:

1. Greet the customer immediately.
2. Give the customer all your attention.
3. Be yourselves with the customer.
4. Act on the customer's behalf.
5. Use and bend the rules to satisfy your customer.
6. Leave your customer with a first-class impression of yourselves and the business you represent.

Using the customer's name

Any person likes to hear his or her name once; but hearing it used twice makes a person even happier. When the customer's name is used in a courteous, friendly manner it has great power to create a good atmosphere by which to start, conduct and complete a business encounter.

Five ways to make the most of opportunities

1. How we deal with customers decides whether we win or lose them. Always look for opportunities to win them.
2. Greet the customer immediately. Make eye contact. Give them all your attention.
3. Act for them. Do more for them than they expect.
4. Build relationships with your customer. Treat them as a real person, not just someone who buys something at your business.
5. Be a special person to your customers. You are unique and so are they, so give them special treatment.

Customers buy for only two reasons

1. To make themselves feel good.
2. To solve a problem.

The reasons people give for buying always fall into either one of these two categories, even though they may be described in many different ways. If people have no problem, no need, they don't buy. If they either don't want to make themselves feel good, or have no need to feel good, they don't buy.

How to sell benefits to your customers

People constantly listen to one radio station which is WIIFM: 'What's in it for me?' That is, whenever we are asked to do something, comment on something or think about something, the subconscious question we always ask is, What will I get out of this? When the perceived benefits are seen to outweigh the perceived disadvantages, we are moved to respond in a positive way. When all we can see are the disadvantages, we respond in a negative way. We are constantly working in our own self-interest.

What's in it for me?

It is a fact of life that people focus on 'What's in it for me?' Customers are interested in products and services that fulfil their wants and needs: products that make them feel good, products that taste good. Customers don't buy products for what they are; they buy them for what they do for them. Last year hardware stores sold thousands of 11-mm drills. No one wanted a drill; what people wanted was 11-mm holes. Last year, too, thousands of upmarket motor cars were bought by customers who not only wanted transport but also wanted the prestige, ego gratification, recognition and superior comfort and safety they were buying, along with the need for transport.

Customers buy benefits

Professor J. Patrick Kelly, who held the K-Mart Chair of Marketing Management at Wayne State University in the USA, is quoted as saying research he conducted on in-store signs indicates that increases in sales of up to 49 per cent can be achieved by the way we price and market our in-store merchandise. Whenever a benefit sign was used on sale items, telling customers how they would benefit from buying the item, it caused a 49 per cent increase in sales turnover. Unadvertised in-store specials with benefit signs caused an increase of 46 per cent. The reason for using benefit price signs is compelling: this type of sign takes account of emotions, which are the major reason the majority of purchases are made.

If the evidence for and the logic of using benefit signs is so sound, does it not follow that we should also be using benefit selling in our everyday presentations to customers? Benefit selling is the most under-used selling skill in this country. Most of us would substantially increase our productivity in selling to our customers if we concentrated on selling benefits.

Here is another example. A salesperson is selling a car, and says, 'A feature of this car is that it has six cylinders and 220 horsepower. This means that you will always have reserves of power when you have to overtake and pass another vehicle. You and your family will be safer because you will spend less time on the wrong side of the road. Overtaking will be a piece of cake. In an emergency you will have the power to keep safe; safety is important to you, isn't it?'

If the customers could express how they would like to be

treated when they are buying, I am sure they would say
something like this:

'*Show me how to get rich. Don't just sell me an
investment program.*'

'*Show me how to enjoy myself. Don't just sell me a
holiday.*'

'*Show me how to develop my career. Don't just sell me
self-improvement.*'

'*Show me how to look beautiful. Don't just sell me
cosmetics.*'

Five ways to sell benefits

1. Focus on the customers — WIIFM (what's in it for me) —
   and then offer benefits to create the wants.
2. Remember, customers want what products and services
   do, not what they are. So turn what they are into what
   they do and you turn the customer on to buying.
3. Learn the difference between features and benefits and
   focus on the benefits.
4. To avoid selling on price, focus on benefits. Show your
   customer why a product or service is great value at a
   certain price because of its benefits. Then list the
   benefits.
5. Customers do not naturally know all the benefits of a
   product or service. We need to become expert at telling them.

What to do when customers object

Every now and then, your customers will raise objections.
Objections or doubts are natural; they are the signposts

that show us the way to creating a satisfied customer. To deal effectively with these objections, it is essential that we do not fear them, but welcome our customers' involvement and use that involvement to make sure they get what they want.

The first principle of dealing with objections is 'listen and learn'. Really listen to what your customer is saying, carefully, attentively and with interest, and you will reduce their objections to part of a process rather than a confrontation. Avoid having confrontations; in a confrontation, you can easily win the fight and lose the war.

There are no smart, sure-fire answers to objections. There are no answers that work all the time; most sales discussions produce some objections. Even in a successful sale, there will be something the customer doesn't like or want. These objections are a valuable part of the selling process. They tell us what progress we are making, and they tell us what our customer is really thinking. Your objective, at all times, should be to satisfy the needs and wants of the customer. You don't have to answer all objections. Some you can ignore. If an objection comes up twice, however, be sure you answer it immediately. If you choose to ignore an objection, be sure you are right to do so, or you will be seen as a hard-sell salesperson.

Five ways to deal with objections

1. Objections are a natural part of a sale. They are telling you what you have to do to make the sale. Welcome them.

2. Listen carefully to the objection and then answer it in detail and ask for confirmation that the customer is satisfied with your answer.

3. Use soft words to answer an objection. For example, 'I understand your concerns, however . . . ', then give your answer. Don't start your answer with, 'Yes, but'. 'But' is a rebuttal and achieves little.

4. Learn and use the 'feel, felt, found' method of answering objections. It is the best non-threatening method I know. It goes like this, 'I can understand how you feel. Many of my customers felt the same way until they found out the benefits they would get from this product. Now many of them tell me it has been one of their best buys.'

5. Your conviction that what you are telling them is the best answer to their problem is the most effective way to deal with objections. Conviction comes only with belief and belief is founded on knowledge, so get to know everything that is important about the products and services you sell.

Five ways to ask for the order

1. Objections or resistance to buying is not a personal issue so don't take resistance personally.

2. Offering alternatives is an easy way to ask for the order. When you have given alternatives, simply ask, 'Which do you prefer?' Now you are asking for the order.

3. Pay attention to buying signals and respond to them by asking for the order, either by alternative questions or a direct question such as, 'Can we proceed with this one?'

4. Timing is critical in all selling. Asking too soon may brand you as being 'pushy'; too late and you may lose the sale. Watch and listen for buying signals.
5. From your opening approach take consent for granted. Always close by using words like, 'When you do this' or 'When you own this'.

When customers complain or are angry

When customers are angry, it is important to understand what has happened to make them angry and what we need to do to make them feel better. Understanding why customers are angry and making them feel better are not the same thing. If they feel bad, this is essentially a problem with human relations. People get angry, upset, defensive, aggressive and difficult, and it is our responsibility to change the situation in which they feel bad to one in which they will feel better. Simply solving the problem of a faulty product, or a failure on the part of the business to do what it promised, may not always overcome the customer's negative feelings. It is possible to fix the problem and still lose the customer, unless we pay a lot of attention to their feelings.

Five ways to deal with complaints

1. Accept that complaints give you the opportunity of strengthening your relationship with your customer.
2. Do not get into a contest. In order for you to win, your customer must win. Forget about who is right. Solve the problem.

3. If you are having difficulties in arriving at a solution, ask the golden question: 'What is it that you think we should do that will solve the problem and be fair to both of us?'
4. Listen patiently, let the customer talk. Ask questions to understand then suggest a solution.
5. Preserving the relationship is the critical issue in complaints. Ninety-five per cent of complaining customers will do business with you again and become more loyal than customers who don't complain if you decide 'now' and in their favour.

Making your business stand out

Every business should never stop trying to make itself different to its competitors, for it is that difference that will draw the customers to you. That is your competitive advantage and if you do not have such an advantage you need to create one.

Have you noticed that many franchise operations work hard at presenting their business premises in a way that says who they are? The McDonald's 'golden arches' is a typical example; probably the most easily recognised premises in the world. Not only do they identify the business, but they also bring to mind what they sell and the service they give. There should be something about your premises that makes it easy for customers to tell their friends how to find you.

When you have achieved easy recognition you should ask yourself other specific questions such as: 'What is the difference between the customer service my business gives and that given by my competitors?' If the answer is, 'I don't know' or 'there isn't any' you have some work to do, because there should be.

When you want to market something, first sell it to someone whose endorsement you and your customers will appreciate. Always ask for endorsements testimonials. This is the most powerful marketing technique you can use. What can be easier than someone else selling your products for you? Watch this technique being used in almost all good marketing. Remember, most humans are followers and act more quickly once they see that other responsible people are already doing what they are now considering. It's good marketing to let customers know that others are doing what you are asking them to now do.

Run sales campaigns

Having a reason for asking customers to buy what you sell is good common sense. It is being brilliant at one of the basics. The advantage of a sales campaign is that it forces you to develop a reason for your customers to buy. A campaign creates some excitement and causes people to take notice of your business. It is a sure-fire way to say to the buying public, 'Here is a business whose management and staff are awake and thinking'. There are hundreds of good ideas lurking in the minds of almost everyone if they take the time and effort to develop them. Why not start by running a 'Develop a Sales Campaign' session with your staff and find out what ideas they have that will help? After all, that is what you are paying them for.

Five ways to market to your customers

1. Search for what makes your business different to your competitors and market that difference.
2. If there is no difference, create one. If you find this difficult then get help. You must find that difference. It's your reason for succeeding in business.
3. Develop a database of customers and make special offers to them. Use pre-emptive advertising techniques.
4. Focus on making your advertising really work for you. Avoid using any ads that don't work. Measure responses from every advertisement. Every advertisement should have a response mechanism.
5. Create response advertising by always asking the customer to: Write to us at____ Phone us on _____ Fax us on _____ Book now by _____ Act now by _____

Focus on the future

All of this is very basic — so basic, in fact, that you may say, 'So what? Everybody knows that.' It is probably true that everyone does know the principles, but most are not carrying them out. Knowing is important, but doing is critical. If you don't do what is needed, there is no value in knowing. Great businesses are great because they do what they know. Ordinary businesses are ordinary because in most cases they are not doing what they know. More especially, there are hundreds of organisations that want to succeed in today's customer-driven marketplace that need to become advocates for the customer.

Here are some of the questions to which you need to find short- and long-term answers because they are critical to your success. Focus on the future of your business by asking:

- Which customers does it serve now and how?
- Which customers will it serve in the future and why?
- Through what channels will it reach them and when?
- Who are its competitors?
- What is its competitive advantage and how can it use it to achieve its objectives?
- What skills or capabilities make it unique and how will it use them to differentiate itself from other like businesses?

The critical issue for all organisations today is differentiation — how a business can make itself different in the perception of its customers — because it is that difference that draws the customer. Your product or service can be obtained from an increasing number of other sources. As a result, differentiation is critical to your future. That differentiation should be based on benefit to the customer because *when your customer wins, you can't lose*. For the age and power of the individual has arrived as never before in our history. Intellectual capacity is our individual bank, our right to work, our passport to financial freedom. Ideas now drive organisations and ideas are the brainchild of the individual. Remember, ideas don't care what sort of idiot gets them, so don't evaluate an idea by who gets the idea. The customer is king and the customer is an individual.

What will be your biggest obstacle to making these changes? The answer, of course, is your thinking. Your greatest obstacle will be your current customer paradigm, because it causes you to see your future as an extension of today. An understanding of paradigms — the dominant mind-sets and patterns that make up our world — is critical to your future, for two reasons. First, you will be faced with an ever increasing rate of change for the rest of your life. Unless you can see the world with new eyes, you may miss your chance. Second, if you are to perform a positive role in the future, you will need to become your own futurist. We try to solve today's problems with yesterday's solutions, and we seek the future by looking through yesterday's eyes. It is not easy to break the habits of the past. It requires persistence and discipline, but it is essential if we are to be successful in this new and different society that is being created. Remember, there is no future in the past and innovation is the way to a successful future.

This is the information revolution and you either join it or it runs over you, or worse still it passes you by. Whatever product or service you sell and however you are currently selling it you can be certain of one truth: it is the best possible obsolete method currently available and you need to find a better and more creative way so that customers will prefer to do business with you.

Fifty years from now, what we are experiencing will simply be a chapter in the history books as a result of yet another major paradigm shift into the future. In the meantime you are not only going to have to live and work your way through these changes, you are going to have to survive, prosper and grow your organisation into a very different kind of organisation which may operate in a very different way. An organisation in which the customer really is king and the central focus of all you plan and do. Remember, *when your customer wins, you can't lose*. There is no future in the past. Today it's innovate or die.

12. Effective Delegation

This presentation was first given to an organisation as part of a complete three-day training program. It was in workshop mode. The audience numbered around twenty and they were all in a management or supervisory position. The key subject for discussion was delegation; the organisation wanted its management to embrace delegation so they could free themselves for more important work that their subordinates could not do. Each and every question posed to the members of the workshop had to be worked through, which took a great deal of time. You can make the best use of this presentation by taking your time and working through each question as if you were attending the workshop.

Mr Chairman, thank you for your kind welcome and introduction. It is my pleasure to share this workshop with you and your people. The key subject today is 'Effective Delegation'. From a manager's point of view effective delegation should be of great benefit because this is one of the management skills that sets the effective manager on the road to success. Some of this workshop consists of answering questions on how managers deal with the issues that make delegation so important. You will get the greatest benefit if you answer the questions truthfully and seek to improve your delegating skills.

Please answer each of the following questions as if you were doing a self-analysis of your current level of delegating skills. Answer in your own mind or, if you are currently reading this session in my book, *Innovate or Die*, write down your answers.

- Who else can do some of the work you could be delegating?
- Do you work long hours, or find yourselves taking work home? If so, why?
- Do you find yourself doing routine jobs others could do, or could learn to do? Why?
- Do you have trouble completing important tasks on schedule because you're doing your work as well as someone else's? If so, why?
- Are you failing to develop your subordinates because you never have the time to train them in more important tasks? If so, why?
- Do you often, or sometimes feel that you are a victim in your position because you cannot complete all the work that needs to be done? If so, why?
- Do you believe that delegating is a sign of weakness? If so, why?
- Do you fear losing control if you delegate? If so, why?

Delegating effectively

If we are to be more successful at our work, we must use the skills and talents of others. Our objective must always be to focus only on top-priority work and to involve ourselves only in the level of work that cannot be done by others. We can't do everything so we need to delegate. Delegating is difficult; it's the hardest thing that managers and executives do.

Here are some of the reasons many of us delegate less than we should

It doesn't occur to us to delegate

We are often so caught up in the act of doing something that it simply doesn't occur to us to get someone else to do it. There is a simple antidote for this: whenever you have a task to complete, ask yourself, 'Can someone else do this?' If so, then get someone else to do it.

We believe it's a sign of weakness

This irrational idea is probably a throwback to our childhood. As infants we come into the world totally helpless. As we mature the parental message to us is: grow up, be strong and learn to take care of yourselves. The image of the totally self-sufficient person may have been valid in an earlier rural society, but in our twenty-first century urban society it is a myth. To delegate is anything but a sign of weakness. Strong managers delegate in order to develop others in their team to a level where they can take much of the load of work from them. This sets them free to plan for the future, which is a key issue today. Not to delegate is to undervalue your most valuable resource: time.

We want to do the work ourselves

Many of us fill our days performing trivial tasks that could easily be delegated. The reason given is usually, 'So what? I enjoy it.' However the enjoyment gained doing less important work is often a way of avoiding the more important issues that we know less about, or that seem less pleasant. It gives us a feeling of accomplishment and quells any guilt or insecurity we feel about ignoring important tasks.

We fear losing control

Insecure managers are a common target for this delegation phobia. Such people fear that if subordinates are trained to perform more duties, they will lose their position to one of them. Like most fears, the fear of losing control is without any real basis and merely holds us back from developing our true potential. If anything, the *failure* to delegate is more likely to result in others being promoted above us.

'I am too busy to delegate'

In many situations, delegation does take time. Time to assign the work and sometimes to train the person and check that the work is done satisfactorily. Like planning, delegating is initially time-consuming but in the final analysis it saves time and energy. By not making the initial investment of time you lose the benefits that can be obtained from becoming an effective delegator and you diminish your ability by hanging on to work that could easily be done by one of your subordinates. Failing to develop them in the long run will only weaken your reputation and success.

'I could do it better and faster myself'

Once again, the problem here is expediency in the short term at the expense of longer range effectiveness. By doing the work yourselves, you are only ensuring that you have to do it again in the future. This excuse also fails to take into account the need to develop the potential of others. By neglecting to delegate, you block their opportunity to learn and grow by doing. Subordinates will look upon a skilful delegator much more favourably than they do those who insist on doing everything themselves.

'No one else has the experience or competence'

If your assistants or employees are incompetent, what are you paying them for? Most of us tend to underestimate what our subordinates and colleagues can do for us. The only way to find out is to give them a meaningful task and let them run with it. It's also the only way they will get the necessary experience to become competent. In the longer term the payoff can be tremendous and can be a very positive plus for your own career.

We want all the credit all the time

In today's competitive workplace it's not uncommon for managers who are driven by the desire to reach the top to do everything themselves. They fear that if those to whom they delegate succeed in a project, the credit will go to them instead of the manager and thus lessen their own chances of promotion. It's always helpful to ask yourself this question: 'If I can't get my subordinates promoted, should I be promoted?' Perhaps we want the admiration and respect of others and by doing everything ourselves, we prove to our friends, relatives, subordinates and colleagues that we are a hard-working, totally dedicated person. Unwillingness to delegate is a common trait among the harried workers. But by not delegating they present themselves with an impossible workload. This is an unhealthy ego trip as well as a great excuse for poor work.

When to delegate?

You should delegate when:

- You have more work than you can effectively carry out yourselves.
- You cannot allocate sufficient time to your priority tasks.
- You want to develop a subordinate.
- The work can be done adequately by your subordinates.

Techniques of delegation

- Delegate at the right time.
- Delegate the right duties.
- Delegate to the right people.
- Sidestep the pitfalls.

Delegate at the right time

The right time to delegate is whenever you can. Begin with minor assignments before you go ahead with the important delegations. There is an important difference between assigning and delegating. When you assign a task you simply tell a worker what to do, you give them instructions with no authority, or room for decision-making. When you delegate you pass on a piece of your authority. You lay down the ground rules of what you want done and the limits of their authority and then you ask them to report when the work is completed.

You delegate when your workload is too heavy and you can lighten your load by delegating some of it to someone else. You delegate before you go away on business trips, or holidays — and it pays to remember how when you came back the organisation seemed to have done better while you were away. Delegate when you take on more work. This usually means changing your priorities and then delegating those that are best able to be passed on to others.

Delegate the right duties

Delegate the right duties, such as activities that continually recur. Delegate routine, delegate lesser details, the lower priority work that frees you to focus on the important issues. Keep asking yourself, 'Which of my regular daily duties can I delegate?' Delegate duties that will develop your subordinates. Delegate duties that will strengthen their individual weaknesses. Delegate a variety of duties that will add interest to their work. Delegate duties that will make them feel important. Let them realise that they could be selected for possible promotions. Delegate duties that will lead directly to promotion. Nothing improves a worker's efficiency and effectiveness more than the knowledge that they are steadily moving towards better things.

Delegate to the right people

Delegate to those who display in their normal work a willingness to take on additional responsibilities. Delegate to those who learn from experience so they can develop their skills. Delegate to those who show leadership qualities. Test them, give them a specific task with all your authority and responsibility to back them up, make the task specific and brief. When they complete it to your satisfaction delegate more important work for them to do. Continue to give increasingly complex and important tasks to them until they reach the level of their current ability, then train them for promotion.

Sidestep the pitfalls

The major pitfall is that once you have delegated your duties you may fall into the danger of neglecting them. Keep track, do not delegate to the point where you lose control of the affairs of your own work. Delegate only after you have completed your plans. Keeping others busy with the wrong things at the wrong time is not the answer. The key is to attend to your own executive duties and delegate your own routine duties where possible. It's the work of your assistants to keep the machine in repair and your work to do the planning and driving.

When you delegate be sure that your subordinates understand

- Why the work needs to be done.
- What they are expected to do.
- The date by which they are expected to complete the work.
- The authority they have to make decisions.
- The problems they must refer back to you.
- The progress or completion reports they must submit.
- How you propose to guide and monitor them.
- The resources and help they will receive in order to get the work done.

Let those to whom you delegate know you don't want any surprises and that you will not tolerate being kept in the dark. That doesn't mean undue interference on your part with the way the work is being done. It is, after all, the results that count. The way it is done can be left to them. Remember always that innovation is the key to success. Give them the opportunity to innovate because innovative workers are the key to a successful future.

Study those to whom you delegate work, test them with problems and encourage their independent thinking, especially their ability to innovate. Expect the best but remember that none of us is perfect. Select those with initiative and back them up when they take the initiative.

Finally, keep track of the delegations you make, show interest in those you select, make time to go through their plans with them, delegate the routine but stay in charge. The hallmark of really successful managers and executives is that they understand that work is never limited but time is. The key issue is increased productivity and one of the major keys to increasing personal productivity is to understand, practise and continually use the art of delegation.

A critical issue in regard to delegating is that we should delegate sufficient of our work so that we can have some time to think strategically and constructively about our part of the organisation. In too many cases executives are so driven by work habits that they rarely have time to be able to think in this way. Today ideas drive every type of organisation and any manager who has no time to think creatively and strategically is really saying that they have no time to do the most important part of their work. Remember, one of the most important roles of an executive manager is to help prepare the organisation for the future because there is no future in the past and today it is innovate or die.

Here is an example of the most effective delegator I have worked with. I was the Marketing Manager of AMP. He was manager in charge of a section of actuaries responsible for technical support for sales and marketing. I needed to get some technical information that would help me in designing a new product for consideration so I phoned him and arranged an interview.

Right on the allotted interview time his secretary came and took me into his office. The first thing that caught my attention was that his desk was free of any work in progress. Nothing at all on his desk. He could see I was a little puzzled. He asked, 'Is something the matter?' I said no, but commented that he had the cleanest desk I had ever seen. He replied, 'Jack, I am paid to manage and that's what I do.' He then asked what he could do for me. I told him what I was trying to do and why I needed help from his department.

He asked a lot of questions and then said, 'Let me tell you what I think you want of us.' Then he described with absolute accuracy what I had told him I needed. He asked, 'Is that what you want us to do?' Then he said, 'When do you need it by?' After I gave him the date he picked up his phone and rang a number and said, 'Allan, would you come in please?' A young man entered the office and we were introduced. Then he said to Allan, 'This is what Jack wants us to do for him. He needs it by [and he gave him the date]. Can you do this for him and deliver by the date it is needed?' Allan asked a couple of questions then replied that he could do the job. Then the manager said, 'Jack, is what Allan is going to do for you what you want?' I replied that it was, and he thanked Allan, who returned to his work.

I received what I needed on time and in the exact format that was needed. I think in terms of delegating we can learn a lot from this manager.

Thank you for your participation in this presentation. Now it is time for each of us to go out into our working world and put into practice the suggestions contained in this workshop, if we are not already doing so.

It has been my pleasure to spend this time with you. I wish you every success.

13. Making Appointments by Telephone

This presentation on telephone techniques was made to a two-day conference of salespeople in New Zealand at which I was the keynote speaker. I have also made it many times at venues throughout Australia. It is a much-requested presentation because in my experience many salespeople find making cold calls very threatening. Perhaps this is because they have not cultivated the techniques that make the telephone user-friendly. In order to be confident of your phone-for-appointments techniques, practise continually by making actual calls using a technique that you are familiar with. Delete those parts that don't work and replace them with what does. Let me begin my presentation.

Mr Chairman, thank you for asking me to make this presentation, it is my pleasure to share this time with you and your people. My presentation today is on making appointments by telephone. Let me begin.

The telephone is either the great communicator or the great time-waster. You must choose. As salespeople it can be a great time-waster or a great time-saver, depending on how well you manage your calls. It is also very important to keep good phone statistics so that you can tell how effective your telephone techniques are. Guessing your statistics can in many cases give you the wrong answer.

Preparation is the key to success in making appointments by phone. Here are the main issues to prepare for:

- Know who to call by name and position.
- Know when to call.
- Know why you are calling — the reason why your prospect should give you an interview.
- Be rehearsed, know what to say and how to say it. Remember, ad-libbing is for amateurs.
- Be prepared for objections and doubts. Have answers ready, for it is probable that you will get some. Know the ones you are most likely to get and prepare and use answers that will effectively solve that problem.

Know who to call by name and position

It sounds elementary, but knowing who to call is the process of matching your offer to a name or position which sparks off that feeling of, 'This is someone who could benefit from my offer, because it will be of value to them for a number of reasons.' Once you are satisfied there is a genuine reason for making the call you only have to have the name of your prospect and if possible their title, or position in their organisation.

Know when to call

Success often comes because your call was made at the right time. For example, it is not much use calling a doctor during surgery hours, or a schoolteacher during classes. It is as well to do some research into the best time for the particular industry or occupation of your prospect. If your sales activities are confined to a narrow section of business activity then you will be familiar with the times your prospect is most likely to be available. If there is any doubt about the right time, make an exploratory call and ask the switch or secretary when the best time would be for you to call, and then name your prospect. Usually you will be given the information; however, you should be prepared to actually make your call because you may be told that your prospect is available now. If that happens, ask to be put through. You may also be asked, 'Can I help?' and you need to have an answer ready. If you sound hesitant or unsure, the normal reaction on the part of the listener is to become suspicious of your motives. Truth and upfront, open behaviour have a power that guile cannot match. If you are asked, 'Can I help you?', say something like: 'Thank you very much for the offer, but you already have by telling me when I am likely to be able to contact Mr Peterson. Would you give him the message that [leave your name] will call him at 9 o'clock in the morning?' When you call, everyone will be expecting you, or at least recall that you have already been in touch. You are now not a complete stranger.

Know why you are calling

This means you need to be able to write a 30-second commercial describing your reason for calling. It should describe in approximately 70 words the benefits that will flow to Mr Peterson as a result of him meeting with you for 20 minutes. Your message needs to have excellent content and the words need to be very descriptive to paint a picture that will lead to your getting the interview.

As an example, I will quote Don Mehlig's telephone appointment approach, which he presented at a seminar and which I consider to be one of the very best I have heard, or read. He is in the financial service industry representing his own business. He thanks Mr Peterson for taking his call, introduces himself and says:

> *Mr Peterson, my purpose in calling you is to arrange a time suitable to you so I can show you how you can benefit from those things your corporation can do for you more effectively than you can do them for yourself taking account of current tax laws. I am sure you would like to know what other successful people in businesses similar to yours are doing to increase their spendable income and after-tax profits. Mr Peterson, are you interested in increasing your after-tax profits and having more money to spend? It will take just 20 minutes to show you how.*

Don says most of his prospects say yes. He also says he has spent a lot of time getting his approach call matched to his market. There are no sure-fire ways that work all the time with every prospect but the more you test and adapt your presentation to the wants, needs and desires of your market, the better your results.

Be rehearsed

We have dealt with building a presentation that will have enough appeal to your prospects to influence them to give you an appointment so that you can make a presentation. Now that you have the story, you need to practise it until it is word perfect. You can then focus on how you say what you have to say. Humans learn by repetition. Champion golfers practise until their swing becomes an automatic response to the need to hit the ball. They depend on their mind reproducing that swing every time they hit the ball, irrespective of the club they are using. Salespeople need to do the same amount of practice on their presentations so they can reproduce their story perfectly every time. This is especially so for phone approaches. For a listener, there is nothing more painful than a salesperson who sounds unsure, indecisive and dull. The response to this kind of approach is nearly always negative. To avoid this problem it is necessary to practise not only the words, but how you say the words. Emotion brings your message to life and is therefore a most important consideration. Knowing what to say is critical but adding emotion to your message really gives it legs.

Be prepared for doubts and objections

You also need to be prepared to answer the doubts and objections given as reasons for not agreeing to your request for an interview. Write down the four most obvious reasons or objections your prospect is likely to make and then write an answer to each and learn them until you are word perfect. This is no time for ad-libbing; be prepared. Ad-libbing is for amateurs. Go back and write your answers to objections and prepare yourselves to respond in a way that will get you the appointment. Keep statistics of your success so that you know whether you need to improve your calling techniques.

Have a 'special' approach to secretaries

Every salesperson makes calls that must go through a secretary and much of the sales training on getting interviews offers techniques for dealing with this so-called problem. In my view it should simply be another process, not a problem. If we think it will be a problem it probably will be. We need to understand that the secretary has the important task of deciding which calls should go through, no doubt on criteria decided by her employer. We should take the realistic view that the objective of the secretary is to make sure we do not get to her employer unless we meet that criteria. We should also assume that her other objective is to be as helpful as possible to those who call. Our objective should be to help her do her work, not create problems for her. After all, if our approach is not considered of sufficient value or interest, that is hardly her fault. If you want to receive better treatment start by giving better treatment.

Be warm, friendly, truthful and treat her as a real person and an equal. When you make the call and the secretary answers she will usually do so by stating the name of the business and giving her first name. In the following example, her name is Helen. Too many salespeople see the secretary as a person who is going to make it difficult for them to get to her boss, the prospect of the call, and they try all sorts of tactics to outwit her. Making it difficult for you to get to her boss is her work, so why not help her do her work and get her co-operation rather than creating conflict?

It's not difficult. When she gives her name, ask her a soft question. Your voice will show that you mean it. 'How are you today?' is a good, friendly, soft question with which to start your conversation. You will be surprised at the reaction you get, because she is rarely asked how she is and will generally reply in a positive way, such as, 'I am well, thank you' and will give you the opportunity to make a further friendly comment. When you make it don't waste time, get on with helping her do her work, but as she has offered her first name, ask her, 'Do you mind if I call you [in this case] Helen?' I have never had a secretary say no to being addressed by her first name.

Then ask: 'May I speak with Mr Peterson please?' When the secretary asks, 'May I ask what it is you want to speak to Mr Peterson about?' reply by saying, 'Yes, you can and I have no objection to telling you what it is. If you can do for me what I need Mr Peterson to do, you will have saved both him and me some very valuable time.'

This is the key issue because now you must state what you want to talk with Mr Peterson about. It must be something the secretary cannot answer for Mr Peterson. Then explain what it is you want from Mr Peterson. If the secretary can't solve the problem she will either put you through if Mr Peterson is available or will undertake to have him call you back if he is not. Now you must choose: a call back to you, or you must call again.

Always choose to call them back and say, 'Thank you for your kind offer but I am moving around and may not be available when he calls. Then I will call him and the same thing will happen and all we are doing is making the phone company rich. What is the best time for me to call Mr Peterson so that we can be sure of getting together?' The secretary will give you a time, say 8.30 in the morning, to which you can reply, 'Helen, if I call in the morning at 8.30 I will be able to talk with Mr Peterson?'

'Yes, you will. I will make sure he is available.'

Now you are getting help, not resistance. When you treat her as a valuable and helpful person she will in most cases respond and treat you as being equally valuable. Always be truthful, open and upfront about what you want. Truth has a power invention cannot match.

Telephone tactics

When arranging interviews, use odd times to gain attention. For example (again, following Don Mehlig's telephone appointment approach), 'Mr Peterson, my purpose in calling you is to arrange a time suitable to you so I can show you how you can benefit from those things your corporation can do for you more effectively than you can do them for yourselves taking account of current tax laws. I am sure you would like to know what other successful people in businesses similar to yours are doing to increase their spendable income and after-tax profits. Mr Peterson, are you interested in increasing your after-tax profits and having more money to spend? It will take just 20 minutes for me to show you how you can achieve this goal. Would morning or afternoon suit you better?'

'Afternoon would be best.'

'How about nine minutes past two tomorrow afternoon? That way we will be finished at 2.30 pm.'

Every time you use an odd number instead of the traditional hour or half-hour times you set yourselves apart from the mob. When you go in depends on when Mr Peterson is ready for you. After pleasantries are exchanged confirm your 20-minute promise by saying, 'Thank you for your time. When I have had my 21 minutes I will tell you and then I am finished unless you ask me to stay. Is that okay?'

When your 20 minutes is up say, 'My time is up unless you want to continue.' If they believe what you have said is important to them they will ask you to continue. If not, leave, because you can always come back if you keep your word. On the way out thank the secretary or receptionist for the help she has given. You may want to come back.

When making your calls

Stand to make your calls; you will become more alert, feel more authoritative and as a result sound more positive and dynamic. Try to identify the personality type of your prospect before you make the call and match your presentation to that type. During the call check if you have made the correct match.

- Relax and focus on a mental picture of your prospect and talk to that picture rather than to the phone.
- Never work while making your call. Only have on your desk information you need to make the call.
- Smile during your call because it immediately causes you to sound more friendly than if you choose to be detached and impersonal.
- Reduce your phone presentation to its simplest, most effective minimum. Be precise. In these days of rush, hurry and complexity, a short, powerful, but simple message is most effective. TV and radio advertisements are mostly 30 seconds or 70 words.
- It is always good practice to ask, 'Is this a good time to speak with you for a few minutes or would you prefer me to call you back?'
- If your call is a cold call be as brief as possible. You are running against their internal human clock and they are always busy and the longer your call the more certain it will cause problems.
- At every stage of your call be polite, even if your prospect is irrational, irritating and non-co-operative. Never display annoyance; it is counter-productive.
- Use words that lead you easily into your presentation: 'My purpose in calling is . . .' 'My reason for calling is . . .' 'I am calling you because . . .'
- Humans usually recall best what they hear first and last. If you give options for consideration always give your preferred option last.

This is not about selling on the phone other than selling the idea that the person you have called should give you an appointment. It is not about your actual sales presentation once you are talking to Mr Peterson — that is dealt with in making a sales presentation. Do not take the telephone for granted. It is not just a piece of modern communication technology, it is a vehicle for first-class communications which if used properly, can greatly increase your sales effectiveness. The phone will do its work well, but it is the user who breathes life into it. The more skilled you are in its use the better your results. Go for it!

Thank you for your attention. You have been a first-class audience.

14. Choose You Can and Choose You Must

This is a presentation I have made many times because it contains one of life's great messages: we are responsible for the choices we make. Even when we refuse to choose, we have made a choice. Every day there are choices that must be made, and if we are not careful we can easily slip into the habit of believing that choosing is not important. Then one day we realise that all those small (and what we thought unimportant) choices we have made have collectively become a mountain of trouble that can no longer be ignored. Let me begin my presentation.

Mr Chairman, thank you for your kind introduction and your invitation to be here to share this time with you and your people. I believe the issues we are about to discuss are critical to each of us at this time, for the world in which we live is undergoing change at a rate never before experienced by the human race. You have asked me to deal with the important issue of choosing, which I will do under the title of 'Choose You Can and Choose You Must'. So let me begin.

Because we have the power to choose we can influence our own destiny. Your choices can make you, or break you. Choice is what separates us from all other known life in the universe within which we live. Choose we can and choose we must, for it is a basic function of life for all of us. None are exempt. From the beginning of life to its end we are choosing. Not choosing is itself a choice. We cannot escape making decisions. Everything is a choice, a decision; choosing not to make a decision is a choice. A major step forward in life is to accept that the decisions are ours and the responsibility for the outcomes of each decision is also ours.

There is no escape from the responsibility of building a life by the choices we make. Even when something happens to us that is completely outside our control we must decide how we will react to what has happened. Will we choose to respond in a positive and determined manner or will we choose to let it influence our life in a negative way and pay the undue interest of worry, anger, sorrow, or some other debilitating attitude of mind that holds us back from making choices that can turn a short-term setback into long-term gain? Thomas Jefferson said, 'Nothing can stop the person with the right mental attitude from achieving their goal: nothing on earth can help the person with the wrong mental attitude.'

It is possible that the event may in fact be a blessing if we embrace the positive possibilities that may now exist as a result. Here is an example of how such an event influenced my life and the lives of my family. I was 31 years old and had a coronary while playing golf in a club competition. At the time I was club champion and it was a stroke event. (No pun intended!) On the second hole I suffered the first pains, which were not strong enough to cause concern. However, the pain became worse the longer I played and at the nineth hole I had to stop playing. By the time I arrived home I knew that something serious was happening. When the doctor arrived the pain had subsided a little, but he said after his examination, 'Jack, I can't believe that at your age you are having a heart attack but I must treat you as if that is the case; so go to bed, be very quiet, call me if you develop increased pain, or develop other symptoms. I will see you early tomorrow.'

Next day I was taken to the hospital for a cardiogram and other tests, which were then sent to Sydney for examination by a specialist. Two days later the doctor told me that I had had a coronary. He told me to stay in bed, no unnecessary moving, be as quiet as you can. I asked him exactly what all this meant and he said, 'Jack, because you are my friend I will tell you exactly what it means. It means that you can die anytime within the next three weeks. If you live for three weeks you'll be okay.' He then explained in detail what had happened to my heart and why three weeks was important.

I remember saying to him, 'What are you going to do for me?' and he replied, 'I'm going to give you these tablets. Take one three times daily.' I then asked whether the tablets would fix the problem and he replied that they were not a cure but they were all he had to give me.

I was 31, married with two daughters; one was three years old and the other nine months old. I had a business that could not operate without me, because I had to prepare the work for others to do. I had just been told I could die any time within the next three weeks and to remember not to worry because worrying wouldn't help my progress. By any measure, that was traumatic news. If I lived I would lose the business and have to start again. If I died, what would happen to my wife and daughters? It was hard to comprehend what had happened. In a few hours my life and the lives of those I cared most about had been turned upside down.

Then something happened to me that is still difficult to explain. The doctor attending me was the partner of my usual doctor who was away on holidays. He was around 60, I was 31, but we were friends and often had discussions of a philosophical nature. I respected him and learned a great deal from him. In all those discussions he gave the impression that he was a little cynical about life and yet here he was, telling me, 'Take these tablets, they are all I have. Live for three weeks and you will be okay.' Then he left and I heard him close the front door and close our front gate. About a minute later he rang the doorbell again. My wife let him in and he came back into the bedroom. He said, 'Jack, there is something else I can do to help you. Do you know how to pray?' I said that I did, and he looked at me for a moment. Then this man that I had always thought was a little cynical said, 'Then pray, son, it is your best chance' and without another word he left.

That evening I prayed and something happened which I find difficult to explain. As I sat in bed and prayed for my family and me, something warm and comforting settled around my shoulders and wrapped itself around me. It was as if someone had placed a warm, protective and comforting cloak around me and as if someone was saying, 'Be not afraid, everything will be all right'. All my cares and concerns disappeared and I was filled with a sense of joy and comfort. From that day the feeling has been with me: divine reassurance and encouragement, not a guarantee, or dispensation, but an assurance that has been as real to me as, 'When you need me, I am here'. Any explanation is simply inadequate so I have accepted it requires no explanation on my part, only faith and acceptance. I am sure some who read these words will understand perfectly because they will have had a similar experience.

I have often wondered what experience my doctor friend had that gave him this spiritual insight and I wondered how many of his other patients benefited from his advice. Perhaps as a result of our conversations he knew that I was on a journey of discovery and he knew his comments would have relevance for me.

Why do I tell you about this event in my life? Firstly, because we did lose our business and we had to start all over again. But out of it came a new and better life. For as I have said before, even in life's darkest hours there is the possibility of better times, of opportunities if we are brave enough to face the dark and troublesome times with faith and look for the good times with courage and conviction. There are always choices we can make that will work for us and not against us.

We chose to start again and to build a bigger and better life. Within five years it had blossomed into opportunities that have brought us success on a scale we could not have imagined in those troubled times. The opportunities and successes are still coming because now I understand how humans can tap into the power greater than themselves and reap the rewards intended for all of us — if we can but understand and accept that the way of all human achievement is through the application of the self-fulfilling prophecy in our life. (I wrote a best-selling book called *Yes*

You Can about this subject.) The power greater than ourselves does not play games, does not judge, but responds always to our thoughts because it is through our thinking that we build our life. As William James, the famous psychologist, said, 'The greatest knowledge of my era is that people can change their life by changing their attitude of mind.'

If we aim to give the best of ourselves at all times, under all conditions, to all people, we are setting standards that will ensure we not only reach our potential but that we also bring happiness and contentment to our life. The choices that we as individuals make will affect others. Our husband, or wife, or partner. Our parents and our children and associates. All life is linked in some way to all other life so we need to be conscious that there are choices that can work for good in the lives of others, that the example of the life we lead can become an inspiration to follow rather than an example to be avoided. And remember: time is life and life is all we have; one chance and it's gone and tomorrow is promised to no one.

Becoming

Humans are forever changing, adapting and moving on, or they are resisting and denying themselves the opportunity of becoming something better. Becoming is critical to each of us: it is the limitless potential of human experience. Just as the masterpiece emerges from the blank canvas of the artist so we can fashion our life by building it in a way that can create the masterpiece we want it to be. As the script of a great play develops from the inspiration and creativity of the playwright, so each of us must write the script for and live out the greatest play of all: our life.

As our life continually unfolds we become the final product of our total expression as a human being. For some it will be a fleeting and forgettable experience, for others it will be the fulfilment of a lifetime of growth and development that will bring a sense of peace and contentment, while always accepting that there is no end to the journey of self-development. Becoming is a constant state of development that only ends when life itself ends as a mortal in this world. Becoming is the act of growing on our journey of potential. For as the universe in which we live and of which we are a vital part is in a continuous state of creation, so must the act of becoming be a continuous growth experience for the individual.

As no two humans are alike, the process and the extent of individual growth will vary for each of us. In nature there are no two of anything exactly the same. In a field of a million wildflowers there are no two flowers exactly alike. That is nature's way of ensuring the survival of the species. If they were exactly the same, a calamity may hit that particular type of flower and all could be destroyed; when each is different the possibility of all being destroyed is limited.

So it is with humans. Even when great plagues swept the world, those individuals who were more resistant to the scourge survived. Even now when disease and drugs sweep through countries like the plagues of old, there are sufficient humans with different values who are not part of that culture. They are different. And it is that difference that will help ensure our species survives yet another challenge.

Becoming is the process of growth within the individual. It is a forever journey, for life is an unfolding experience and will be so for as long as we live. Even if the only experience of change we have is to grow older we cannot escape the changing nature of life itself. For some, becoming as a process of life will be a wonderful experience full of accomplishment, joy, happiness and fulfilment. For they will have a definite plan to explore their potential to the fullest, not with the goals of being the most successful, richest, or most powerful human in their sphere of influence — although that is possible if that is their desire — but more to accomplish the goal of understanding self and becoming whole in the sense of knowing with certainty who they are and why they are here. For them, the search for meaning in a changing world will have been accomplished. For others it will be the opposite: a journey of problems, fear, worry and uncertainty. A life with no real purpose. A series of haphazard stops and starts driven by no set pattern. It is so easy to get involved in the sideshows of life and fail to reach our true potential.

The question of why we are here, what is the purpose of human life, has always been the biggest. The answer, as I see it, is that the purpose of life is life itself. We are here to learn and to grow as a human being so that the purpose of human existence can be accomplished. We will not live long enough to see that happen, but our task is to make progress while we are here and if we can say at the end of our time that we have done our best, then our journey will not have been in vain.

Becoming is more than an acceptance that whatever happens to us is meant to be. If we are to just accept life as it comes without exerting any real influence over events, then our life may never become the positive, rewarding and happy event that it has the potential to be. It is so easy to become an observer of life instead of being a participant. To observe we only have to see life as if it is happening on a movie screen, as if it is happening to someone else. It does not seem real, so there is no need to be upset or concerned, but if our life is to have meaning and purpose we need to become involved. To become a participant it is necessary to become involved, interested and to know the rules of the game, for being involved is an essential part of becoming.

Becoming is about growth and change. It is the acceptance that life is the challenge. The challenge of growing and becoming a better person, of developing a deeper understanding of what is worthwhile; of accepting that we are exchanging on a day-by-day basis one day of our life for whatever we are willing to take in return. One of the great truths of life is that each day we take one day of a life and trade it in the marketplace for whatever we are willing to take in exchange for the day we are trading. It would seem important that what we receive in return is at least worth what we give. It would be devastating to find at the end of our journey that what we have exchanged our life for has not been worth the life we gave.

To become what you want to be is a challenge worth the effort required. Use whatever powers you have to influence the course of events in your life to reach your desired destination. You have the power to make the right choices; you were not created to live out a life decided in advance by anyone, or anything. You do have free will and you are in charge of your own destiny. To believe the opposite is to say, 'It doesn't matter what I think or feel; my life has already been decided. All I must do is go through the process of whatever is to happen to me.'

To believe that is to believe that some are chosen by divine providence for all that is great and glorious while for others it will be despair and suffering. That would mean that life is a matter of luck, either good or bad. To accept that is to deny our maker, who has given us everything we need to be everything we want to become. Each of us was born with all we will ever need to accomplish all we want to become. There is no limit to what you were given: a divine gift with one condition attached. You have to discover it within yourselves and bring it into your own life. No one else can give it to you because like you they can only find it for themselves.

You were also given the means to bring what you want into your everyday life through the power of the self-fulfilling prophecy which is at work in your life, every second of your existence. It is the way of all human accomplishment and the source of divine power given to each and every one of us the day we were born. Today there are millions of people worldwide, from every walk of life, discovering and using this great power in their life. If you are to become what you want, you must learn to use and direct this power to create the life you want and to bring you unlimited happiness, success and wealth.

The process we adopt to take us on our journey of becoming will differ from person to person and so the results will also differ for each of us — from outstanding success to disappointment. For some it will be a constant state of confusion and chaos.There will be times when we ask questions like, 'Why me? What did I do to deserve this?' Both questions imply that someone or something else is responsible for our life and that we are just playing a role and have no control over our destiny. It would be more productive if we were to accept that we are in charge and that by our thinking we create the life we have. Once we do so, we are able to ask the right question, which is, 'How can I give myself the best chance of achieving a successful outcome in my search for self and becoming who I want to be?' It is here that all who face the challenge have common goals, for the attitudes, skills and habits that win for one will win for all. The only difference will be in your level of application. If you want a lot you have to give a lot, but if you want little then you will have to give little. Becoming financially independent is no different. It is a case of setting the goal and then going after it with purpose and passion.

Becoming is the act of changing from what you are, to what you can become, through self-development applied in a constructive and continuous way. It is the outcome of your thoughts through the power of the self-fulfilling prophecy. The key attitudes that will help you build the life you want and become the person you want to be are:

- The vision you have of the life you want.
- The involvement and application you are willing to contribute.
- The dedication and persistence you apply to getting it done.

Let's look at those three issues.

The vision you have of the life you want

Whether you are aware of it or not, you currently have a vision of your life. It may be bright and strong, or weak and blurred. It may be a goal that is real and on which you are constantly working in order to bring it to fruition, or it may be no more than a constant daydream which you accept will never come true. However you see it, the truth is that what you think will be what you become and by your thinking the decision is constantly being lived out as reality in your life. If you want to create wealth in your life and become financially independent then it must become a goal that burns brightly in your imagination. See yourselves achieving your goal, step by step. When it becomes fixed in your mind and you believe beyond all doubt that you will make your dream come true, it will no longer be part of your imagination, it will become fact in your life.

Your vision of the life you want is critical to its achievement. You should take the time to explore your present thinking and make certain that you are heading in the direction of the life you want. Now is the time to examine your values system to ensure that what you believe, is consistent with what you are trying to achieve. If you want your life to be an example of all that is noble and beautiful then your actions need to be based on those same values. If truth, compassion, fairness and love for your fellow man are important to you then they must be reflected in your vision. For what you think is what you get.

The involvement and application you are willing to contribute

See it brightly in your imagination, for that is the first step to its attainment. Make it the important goal it deserves to be. Set out a plan of action that in general terms will take you in the right direction and then constantly monitor your progress. Life is an unfolding process and if you are constantly adjusting your direction so that it mirrors your vision you can be certain you will get the right result. Great goals do not happen by accident; they are the result of a creative action plan that is carried out in a logical, consistent manner. See my presentation on 'Goal-achieving' (Chapter 10 of this book) and follow that system. It is the best available.

The dedication and persistence you apply to getting it done

This is not an easy task. It requires total commitment and a constant awareness of whether what is happening is going in the right direction. Above all, it requires the strength of purpose to make the hard decisions when your plan gets off track. Few plans go perfectly, most experience some difficulties and generally it is at these times that we win or lose. All of our lives impact on the lives of others and in turn what they do affects us. When decisions have to be made that do affect others, difficulties can arise.This is the time when we are most likely to compromise our vision and we need to be certain we are willing to pay the price of that compromise and alter our vision accordingly.

The wider picture

Becoming is a lifelong process of change but it doesn't mean you have to wait a lifetime for either success or happiness. You may have achieved both of these goals in a short space of time and it is only a matter of the degree of success, or happiness you continue to work for. Irrespective of the outcome of your efforts, there will always be change taking place within you and around you. The process never stops until we die — and even then we have to learn how to die for the first time. The end of our life may be the time when we will undergo the greatest change and achieve the most progress.

While looking at the positive side of what we are to accomplish if we are to become what we want to be, it is necessary to acknowledge that we don't all start as equals. Some are born into affluence and position while others are born into poverty and despair but few if any of us are born without hope and the opportunity to improve our lot. History shows us that many of those born to affluence and position finished in poverty and despair, while many of those born with burdens that would defeat most blossomed under the challenge and became role models for all to follow. Many of those who undergo horrific accidents take charge of their life and become wonderful examples of the way the human spirit can overcome any challenge. There is no limit to becoming, other than that imposed on ourselves by ourselves. While ever the divine spark flickers within us, so hope burns and the opportunity to become something better flourishes.

Focus on choices that will build your life in a positive manner. Humans are the only known species in the universe who have the power to choose, so choose wisely, because life itself is only the sum total of the choices you make. Remember, every decision is a choice. Not choosing is a choice. We cannot escape choosing. To increase your chances of winning in life be careful what you choose. Focus on the fact that the following three choices will have the most impact on your life.

Firstly, choose to associate with positive can-do people of good standing and deny the negative people of this world, for your choice will impact on your life.

Secondly, be choosy about what you read and see. Make sure you focus on the positive can-do side of life and avoid the degrading and negative aspects of life, for what you see will influence your life.

Thirdly, be choosy about what you hear. Listen to what will develop you in a positive manner and avoid the negative aspects of so much of what we hear.

These three issues decide whether you win or lose. Remember that each day we trade one day of our life in the marketplace we call life for whatever we are willing to take in return. At all times make sure you get value for what you trade, for it may impact on your life forever. You can't have your life over again. You can only make sure you choose wisely. Choose to be an innovative and persistent performer, for remember there is no future in the past; today it is innovate or die.

Thank you for listening. Go in peace and be kind to yourselves and those you love and care for. Build your life into what you most want. Don't hold back. Give it all you've got. You come this way but once: it's now or never.

15. Commitment and Fulfilment

This presentation was given to an audience of over 200 salespeople and their managers. I was asked to define why many salespeople do not reach their full potential, and why it is difficult to get them committed to their own and to the organisation's goals. The presentation was to be motivational and inspirational and introduce new ideas and attitudes that would also inspire the managers to develop new ways of managing their teams. It is also necessary for both managers and their salespeople to accept that hard work and an expectation of winning play a major role in achieving success. Let me begin my presentation.

Mr Chairman, thank you for your kind introduction and your invitation to be here to share this time with you and your people. I believe the issues we are about to discuss are critical to each of us at this time, for the world in which we live is undergoing change at a rate never before experienced by the human race. You have asked me to deal with the important issue of 'Commitment and Fulfilment'. So let me begin.

In order to accomplish our desire for fulfilment we need to be successful in achieving what we desire most in our life.

We need to get what we have been working for. It could be more money, more time, more excitement, more freedom, more ego recognition, more travel, more independence, more love and caring. Perhaps none of these things, but without the desire for something there is no need to achieve anything. Be very clear in your mind what you want to achieve because the brighter it burns in your mind the more certain it is that you will achieve your dream. Whatever you want to accomplish, it is your responsibility to achieve it. No one owes you anything. Not your work, your boss, your wife, or husband, or partner, or your family. All of those people may be willing to help you get what you want, but the ultimate responsibility is yours.

Why do so many not get what they want? Mostly because they are not totally committed to their goal. They dream more than they act; they are really not totally committed.

Ask yourselves these questions to discover how you rate in this business of being totally committed to achieving what you want from life:

- How long is it since you worked seven days and nights to get a goal, to win?
- How long is it since you have achieved a goal against great odds, to win?
- How long is it since you have done something at great personal inconvenience in order to achieve a goal to which you were committed?

There is no prize for having done these things — there is only the hope that you recognise commitment is the key to winning in life. Commitment is the result of and the evidence of strong motivation. Once we are motivated sufficiently to become strongly and totally committed to an ideal, a vision, a dream or an objective, then we can give our all to its achievement. Commitment is the key issue. It is the bond you have with yourselves. It's your personal contract to get the job done. To win. It's the difference between talking and acting. Commitment is the fire you light within that won't go out, no matter the difficulty. It is a fire that can only be extinguished by the achievement of the goal to which you are committed.

Commitment is everything; without it we are at best lost souls who wander the world seeking a place. We invent goals to which we are not committed. We dream dreams to which we have no commitment. We make plans to which we have no allegiance and invariably they languish and die through lack of commitment and we fail to win. Those who are the world's winners are different: they really do march to the beat of a different drum. They are the ones who know the rules, they have a system, they apply a method, they are committed to winning. They daydream as the basis of decision-making, they decide. They plan as a basis of accomplishment, they make it happen, they win.

How then can we accomplish what they know and do? We can accomplish it by first understanding the process, by understanding why we behave as we do. With understanding comes the possibility of motivation, with strong, powerful motivation comes desire and with desire comes commitment. From commitment comes action. From action comes results, rewards and further motivation and we win more often. Then the cycle of winning is complete, it becomes the winner's way. But sadly, not for all. Many spend their time on the lowest rungs of life's ladder waiting, hoping, longing for the chance. The chance that so often never comes because life's not like that. Good things in life don't happen by accident, they happen on purpose. They happen according to a plan. Winning is not an accident, winning is planning our lifetime goals and going after them with every talent at our disposal. That great motivator Vince Lombardi said, 'Success is a day-by-day, inch-by-inch struggle towards one's goals.' Denis Waitley once said to me, 'We achieve our dominant thought.' It would seem that Lombardi and Waitley are in harmony. Waitley is saying we achieve our common most dominant thought and Lombardi says that success is the day-by-day, inch-by-inch struggle towards our goal. I am saying that if we define our goal and make it our common most dominant thought we commit ourselves to our inch-by-inch, day-by-day struggle towards our goal.

Let me give you the secret of how you can achieve your goals. It is guaranteed to work — if you work the plan. This is the secret of how it works. Believe that it works. Trust the method. Understand that life is a self-fulfilling prophecy so start thinking every day of what it is that you want. Understand that you can only move towards what you want, not away from what you don't want to be or achieve, so focus on what it is you want to do, or want to become. Make it your common most dominant thought because day by day each day we achieve our most dominant thought. Then enact your commitment; no rest until it is done. Nothing is too tough, nothing is too difficult; nothing will stop you accomplishing this goal.

Then it is done: the goal has been won. The pleasure of achievement. The satisfaction of winning. The reward of accomplishment. All made possible by commitment. Commitment, as I see it, is the key issue, it is the driving force that makes it impossible to rest until the goal is won. Yet it seems to be the ingredient so often missing in the make-up of so many people. Perhaps it has something to do with today's quality of life because there seems to me to be an ever growing confusion in trying to marry together the concepts of the quality of life with goal-achieving and commitment to objectives. Too often it seems that the goal-achieving and objectives lose out to the quality of life. It is not my purpose to tell you how you should run your life, but it is my purpose in this section to raise your awareness of some of the reasons why performance doesn't always naturally follow desire. Because desire without commitment is of no use.

Go to my presentation on 'Goal-achieving' (Chapter 10) and you will find the world's best goal-achieving method. Use it to define, control and direct your activities till your goal is won.

Here are some of the things I have learned in my journey through life. I have learned that with few exceptions people will help when help is needed. That the world is our oyster, that each one of us can in fact do and become whatever we want to do, or become; that the only limiting factors are those we place on ourselves. There is no obstacle that we cannot overcome if we want to badly enough.

I have learned that creative thinking and thinking differently pay highly. That the world pays a higher price to those who are willing to think differently and constructively.

That expressing oneself differently is important. Today it is innovate or die.

I have learned from all types of people who have given me all sorts of examples, mostly through their own personal achievements, that life really is a self-fulfilling prophecy and that the greatest sin one can commit against oneself is to not be prophetic. That success invariably follows hard work, persistence and dedication, and that the greatest winning edge any human being can have is to be a positive, enthusiastic, self-motivated, highly committed individual. I have observed and learned that adversity at some time or other strikes most of us and that the strong grow stronger and the weak wither away. When observing others, I have learned that there is nothing too tough to stop some people and it's just as obvious that some are simply not strong enough to withstand anything. That people nearly always see things from their individual point of view and that we, being individuals, always see it from our own point of view.

I have learned that life is a compromise and the most successful people are those who know when to compromise and what compromise to make. Like many others, I have learned that issues are very rarely black and white as we tend to believe, but are mostly in the middle greys. I have learned that trying to do all things and be all things is a very tough job and that if you don't know where you are going, it doesn't matter which road you take. Remember, there is no future in the past.

So I say to you that if you want a greater measure of success than you now enjoy, if your objective during the coming year is to get more, see more, do more, or have more — whatever you want more of, whether it's time, money, recognition, travel — your chances of getting it are better if you can identify what you want, decide when you want it and agree what you will give in return for what you get. There are no free lunches.

Then set a plan and do it. If you can identify such a plan, if you can commit and see it through with enthusiasm, then you've got it made. Remember, commitment is the key, winning is the fulfilment. Like me you will have heard the statement many times that ideas are a dime a dozen, but let me say again that the ideas you have and don't use are no more effective than the ideas you have never had and couldn't use.

Selling is no mystery. There is no mystery about what makes sales divisions run. The fuel that fires sales systems is marketing, advertising, salesmanship, motivation, inspiration and support, and you and I have a vested interest in all of those factors; indeed, they are the very basis on which a system of selling is founded. They are the basis on which the life and growth of our businesses are founded. Marketing, advertising and salesmanship. You and I apply the fuel that fires the sales system and as long as we supply it in abundance that system will grow and succeed.

The final ingredient to make it all possible is time. Time to make it all happen. As you sit here today you have the time. Twenty-four hours of the day, the same as every other person on earth, including those on either side of you and every other person at this conference. What you do with it depends on what you believe. If you are still labouring under the false impression that time equals money, let me bring you enlightenment. Time does not equal money, time equals opportunity. Work equals money and the higher the quality of work and thinking you do in the available time you have, which is the same amount as all others on earth, the more money you will have. If you want to test my theory, if you believe that time equals money, then stop work for the next year and let me know at the end of the year how much money you have made. It shouldn't be a very long conversation once you have stopped crying. In absolute terms, time guarantees only one thing and that is decay.

Today you have the time and today you have the opportunity of this new year; now you must make the decision as to whether you get deeply involved, committed and organised to succeed. My view is that the opportunity you have here today and don't take will be no more productive than any other opportunity you had and didn't take. All of this, the pursuit of goals, the attainment of productivity, is really simply a matter of commitment. A desire to want to do better. An understanding that one really must progress or go backwards.

Here is some simple advice. Get your thinking right so you can get on with the job. Set your goals in the following manner. Write them down, make them as realistic as possible. Too high and you become discouraged; too low and you starve to death. Then check them daily, weekly, monthly and quarterly until you have achieved your overall goal.

Getting your goal is just as simple as that. Make it a priority, set aside the time to get it done and stick to the job with unwavering dedication and absolute commitment. It is vitally important that each of us has goals. That we have planned our destination. No ship leaves a port without a destination. Joe Powell, one of the markets great motivators, says in a training program that when a ship misses the harbour it is never the fault of the harbour. I am saying that if you don't know where you are going it doesn't matter which road you take.

Perhaps some stand aside and do not become involved for reasons most of us have, which can be traced back to fear of failure. Most of us never really get to understand that we can be a lot better than we are, that almost anything is within our reach. Others among us perhaps are not getting involved because they are not sure whether the goal they seek is within this job. Let me assure you that the greatest time of your life awaits you here and now if you want it enough. Understand that if you make it the time of your life, you can have it. Denis Waitley remarked to me, 'The opportunity we see, the reward we want, is here in the job we now have if we will only recognise it.' I am saying that if we can get our head into gear, set ourselves realistic productivity goals, recognise that it is work and not time that will bring our goals to reality, then, my friends, we will enter into a truly new era of opportunity, happiness and prosperity. A wonderful opportunity to serve — and we can do that best by understanding that today the greatest unsatisfied need in the community is the one for which there is limitless demand; it is the desire for satisfaction. Give it and you become great. Remember, commitment and persistency are a powerful pair. It is said that Lincoln failed 10 times and then became President of the United States. Edison failed 200 times to make his lamp work and then he lit the lamp that has lighted the world ever since. Lincoln and Edison were committed to a dream, an idea and an objective of winning. It is my hope that you will follow their example and through commitment you will achieve fulfilment.

I hope in some small way I have helped you to light your light, to see your way a little clearer, to kindle in you a flame that burns a little brighter. A fire of commitment to winning that you can only extinguish by the satisfaction of your personal achievement of your own goals. Remember, there is no future in the past. Today it is innovate or die.

I wish you every success.

16. Striving For Excellence

This was a presentation I made to an audience of champion salespeople. As an elite team they were world-class leaders in their occupations. I had been retained to challenge them as individuals to not only meet the target requirements necessary to qualify for attendance at a special offshore conference, but to exceed the requirements of qualification and by their example lead the way for others to follow. That challenge has passed, but their winning response to the challenge is now part of their organisation's history during a time of great change. We should take Elaine Maxwell's advice when she said, 'My will shall shape the future. Whether I fail or succeed shall be no man's doing but my own. I am the force; I can clear any obstacle before me or I can be lost in the maze. My choice; my responsibility; win or lose, only I hold the key to my destiny.' Let me begin my presentation.

Mr Chairman, thank you for your kind welcome to your conference and for your invitation to make this presentation. Let me remind you that school is never over for those who want to survive and prosper in this new and different marketplace. There is no future in the past. Today my subject is 'Striving for Excellence'. Let me begin.

Ulysses spent 10 years of his life striving against great odds to return to his home and his family. Ten years before he achieved his goal. Ten years of constant striving on what seemed to be an endless journey in pursuit of his goal. I offer you not the challenge of 10 years, but that of two years in which to qualify and attend this great summit and during that time to take up a new challenge, which is to not only attend the summit, but to qualify at levels higher than those required to achieve attendance. My purpose during this presentation is to challenge you to achieve those higher levels.

As I understand it, there are three very good reasons why you should strive to attend this particular summit; three very good reasons why you should also consider qualifying at higher levels than those necessary to attend. The first is to ensure that we perpetuate the system under which we live and work; the second is to recognise and promote elitism in your group as a method of achieving that first objective and the third is to satisfy your own personal need for self-achievement and satisfaction, the need to perform at an elite level.

Recognise the benefits of the free enterprise system

It is important, indeed imperative, that each of us recognises that the system under which we work is the capitalist free enterprise system. It is the one that best functions for us in our work as salespeople. Indeed, it is the only system that offers us the kind of opportunities we seek in our work. We tend to forget — in fact some seem never to learn — that the real opportunity we derive from the free enterprise system is that it allows us to work harder. It guarantees us the right to do more, to get more, it preserves our right to receive the benefits that flow from that extra effort. We must always strive to preserve that right and the best way to do that is to reach higher levels of accomplishment.

It is important to understand that in our day-to-day striving for achievement, the opportunity to improve ourselves will be lost if the free enterprise system which produces the opportunity fails. We need to recognise that we, those people who enjoy it most, must make sure that the system prospers and is perpetuated. I imagine that there are some here today who, like others, are concerned about quality of life, whatever that means to each individual. I guess that in my own way I am just as concerned. To me, quality of life starts with an understanding of the system that has made it all possible and of the necessity of preserving that system for the benefit of ourselves and our children. If we do not take this opportunity that the system offers, if we who value it most and who benefit most do not work harder because the system allows it, then we are failing the system and as sure as night follows day the system will collapse. The only real defence we can mount is to strive to make it work successfully. We need to understand that the free enterprise system gives us this right and we are the ones who must make it work. Those who understand this situation have and are promoting this wonderful summit as one of the pleasurable ways of achieving our personal goals, and at the same time fostering our endeavours to keep the free enterprise system working.

Now more than ever before we must be aware of and accept the obligation to perform in a way that will facilitate the system so that its benefits flow to us. It is not good enough for us to be concerned only in a political way, it is not good enough for us to be active only when danger threatens; the real way to avoid both those situations is to take the opportunity that the system offers. To work harder, achieve more, generate the profits, foster among all we meet the understanding of the free enterprise system. Each one to teach one. Strive to not let a day go by when we do not in some way bring this awareness to other people. And when the question of the quality of life arises, it is best we remember that the major benefit that flows from this system is the opportunity to work harder.

The opportunity to do less is in broad terms setting up failure. The one opportunity that is denied under most other systems is the opportunity to work harder and attain more. Most rely on reducing people to a common denominator; we do not want that kind of system. Now I am for free enterprise and it's better to be for something than against something. If we do not support our system then some other system will grow and take its place.

We are not born with an innate understanding of the free enterprise system. We can learn another 'ism' just as easily and we can believe in it just as much, we can enjoy it just as well and we can strive for it with just as much conviction. All around us we see countries changing because more people in that country are learning another 'ism'. That is a simple observation. I offer it as the reason we should take the opportunity that the summit offers and run with it. None of the alternative systems will offer similar opportunities. It is useless to pretend that it can't happen to us. If you cast your mind and memory back you will recall that over the last 30 years we have seen a decline of some nations as major forces in the world. Expressed in broad and simple terms, this seems to have been brought about because they misunderstood the role of the free enterprise system and they traded it for another 'ism'.

When assessing the effectiveness of the system it is important for us to remember that only a few hundred years ago a group of people in a small boat called the *Mayflower*, seeking their new world, landed in a strange country and, as Joe Powell put it, they forged an axe, chopped their way to Pittsburgh, cleared a continent and in the shortest time in history they became the most powerful nation on earth. Either by accident or design they adopted the free enterprise capitalist system and they sold their way to nationhood. Most likely because they were not restricted by any system, they followed what seemed the best way to get results for themselves as individuals.

We in Australia came under a different motivation. Forced to seek our new world, we were largely compelled to migrate and in our early years the system under which we lived was anything but free enterprise. However, once given the chance to work and grow, we accepted the opportunity and with sweat and muscle we built the nation we are today.

There is no mystery about what makes the system run, the fuel that fires the free enterprise system is marketing, advertising and salesmanship and you have a vested interest in all three of those factors. Indeed, they are the very basis on which our own enterprise is founded. Marketing, advertising and salesmanship. We supply the fuel that fires the system and as long as we supply it in abundance the system will grow. That's why it is so important to you and me that we not only understand the basic principles but that we understand why it is important for us to be better at our work. Why winning results are so necessary, why striving for the summit is our role. When we ask ourselves, 'Should we strive for the summit?' we should at least know that the decision we are making is very important. It is not only a question of whether we will be at the next summit; it is basically a question of whether we will perpetuate free enterprise as a system, as the way we want to work and the lifestyle we want to follow.

Recognise and promote healthy elitism

A second way of purposefully achieving our objectives to strive for the summit is to embrace elitism as a vehicle to make it happen. In describing a solution to a problem which he saw as a major problem besetting his nation, Lord Hailsham, a leading British political figure of the twentieth century, said that elitism was the reason why England became great. He said that in every field of endeavour success depends upon excellence, and excellence is most successfully pursued in the company of others following the same objective. He went on to say that education, training, inspection and discipline are the necessary conditions for successful achievement. In material terms, he felt that England needed to go back to the time when 'made in Britain' was a guarantee of quality. When an Englishman's word was his bond. When British justice was such a sure guarantee of fair play and dispatch that merchants all over the world stipulated English law as their authority and English courts and English judges the arbiters of their disputes. His country needed to go back to the days when London was a synonym for financial integrity and commercial efficiency, when people could rely on the quality of craftsmanship and the acceptance of the binding character of promises, whether legally enforceable or not. It was his belief that there was no other salvation for British industry. He said, 'Elitism is the leaven in the bread, the salt in a dish, the thing without which life is flat, stale and unprofitable. It is the pursuit of excellence in all its forms and without it we will perish.' In this statement we have a great statesman striving to show his nation the way out of its problems.

Now we in our organisation are fortunate that we have no need to go back to where the British once were because that is where we stand today. Our organisation in our country represents all that is good, all that is secure, all that is worthwhile and all that is dependable. We are in the situation whereby being backed by our organisation is a sure guarantee of quality. There has never been a time when the word of our organisation, disseminated through its management and its salespeople, was not a guarantee of fair play. All who deal with us know that we have a great name for financial integrity and commercial efficiency. We are the standard by which many others are judged. When we sell our product it literally means you can buy it with every confidence. We are proud of how we do that part of our work.

But the objective is to strive to do more, not less. Less is not the answer. If we are to continue to flourish it can only be because the good we do and the good we have is seen and owned by the people who deal with us. The pursuit of excellence is an objective that we should be actively concerned with at all times and striving to reach the summit can be a means of obtaining that objective.

You represent the top 10 per cent of your sales organisation. You are an elite team and the function of that team is to set the pace, build the standards, stay ahead of and lead the masses. By doing that you become a force which, by its example, determines our progress. You are the elite. By any standard, you as individuals make up an elite team. You are the leaders in an enterprise that leads its own industry in a fashion superior to any other similar enterprise in the world. We have no need to go back. Forward is our only challenge; we are striving to meet the future and to continue to make progress. You need to understand the significance of your role. Understand how important it is for you as the leader to make rapid progress. To be the leader is your proper function, striving to achieve excellence should be your constant endeavour, and retaining that objective should be your absolute commitment.

Within our organisation you are the elite who have moved on to raise the standards of the whole organisation and to aim to be the best in the insurance world, challenging others and striving to reach new levels of performance for no other reason than because you are a member of an elite team. I can only say that I am proud to be with you here today. I know that you understand the obligation that goes with achievement and I am encouraged that you will understand and accept this challenge of striving for the summit and that you will see that attaining the summit is your proper role.

Satisfy your personal need for achievement

If you do not want to accept either of those reasons as one that will move you to strive to reach the summit, then think about it from your own personal view and how it affects you as an individual. Striving to achieve excellence and to make progress has to become as natural to you as breathing. Ever since man stood upright and walked he has been striving to fulfil his destiny, always searching, always changing, always improving, always challenging. We're not exploring space simply because it seems a good thing to do; we're exploring space because there is nowhere else to go. We are fulfilling our quest and striving to unlock the riddle of the universe and man will not be denied that satisfaction. When we were born, our maker planted this desire to do better in our breast and man will not be denied that fulfilment. To deny it is to deny our whole purpose and existence.

Yet always along the way there are those who have wanted to opt out, to stay put, not because they think we have fulfilled our destiny, but rather because it suits them. Today, as legitimate as those pleas may sound, they are simply advocating that we self-destruct as a civilisation. There is no doubt in my mind that the human race will not only adapt and cope, but enjoy, foster further achievement and move on, whatever our level of advancement. Growth and change have always caused problems and will do so in the future. Human achievement has often suffered from temporary defeat; as an example Edison is said to have failed 200 times to make light work and then he lit the lamp that has lighted the world ever since. Edison achieved his destiny. Ulysses strove for 10 years against all odds and then he returned and fulfilled his destiny. Will you be denied yours?

Do you want to get off and continue to produce at the level you now do, or do you accept my challenge to strive for the summit? Do you want to strive to achieve these new levels and qualify for new rewards and set new goals? Will you accept the challenge I give and strive to fuel the free enterprise system and sustain it for ourselves and our children? Will you strive to enjoy and foster elitism as a way to provide that fuel? Will you strive to understand and accept that you have within you all that is needed to keep us great and make us even greater? You can sustain others by your success and by so doing assist each of us in our own small but significant way to fulfil our destiny — and we will walk a little taller because of your achievements. Will you answer my challenge? Will you strive to make the summit? Remember, there is no prize for achieving all these ambitions other than the pleasure you get and the self-fulfilment of your role as the champion sales team you are.

It has been my pleasure to spend this time with you. May you enjoy the fruits of your efforts because you deserve them. May success be yours every day of your life. I wish you well.

17. Beating Your Own Best Performance

This is a presentation I gave to an audience of salespeople and their managers. The organisation that retained me to give this presentation was concerned that their sales division was having a tough time absorbing all the changes that were taking place in their market. The salespeople's concerns were that it seemed they would be doing more work to achieve their normal financial return. For most of them it would mean adopting new methods and setting new goals, using time more effectively and, above all, beating their own previous best performances. If you are not a salesperson but are involved in any other management discipline, I suggest you adopt the same principle of beating your own best performance.

Mr Chairman, thank you for your kind welcome and your invitation to be part of your conference. My key subject today is 'Beating Your Own Best Performance'. Let me begin. Deciding your strategy and direction will be critical to your success; so give them the time and attention they deserve. These issues are too important to leave to chance, and business-as-usual is not an option because business as it used to be is gone forever.

Today competition is swift and tough. The standards needed to do business in this new market environment are going to be higher if you want to taste the pleasures of success — and success in plenty will be there for those who are willing to meet the standards of this new marketplace. Richard Needham offered some good advice when he said: 'Strong people make as many mistakes as weak people. The difference is that strong people admit their mistakes, laugh at them, learn from them. *That is how they become strong.*' The focus is now on what the customers want to do; they are saying 'Change your attitudes, behaviour and products to what we, the customers, want.' The result will be that the customer will buy more and those among you who meet your customers' emotional needs as well as their financial needs will prosper in a way that currently may seem impossible. Don't fight it, change it. Think back and remember how we responded to some of the proposed changes of the past. Then reflect on our fears and concerns at that time and consider the results of those changes. Nothing dramatic happened except things were better after the changes occurred.

The days are gone when big business can sit out the discomfort of change. We see it every day: the dinosaurs of business meeting the inevitable fate of all those who resist change and who lose sight of the customer. The great truth of change and competition is that it is generally promoted by the customer. Remember, to adapt is to follow; to create is to lead. To focus on the customer is to understand the best way of finding a successful solution. Remember, the customer is the doughnut and not adhering to what the customer needs and wants is the hole. So focus on the customer as your way to prosperity.

I predict a time of unparalleled progress and prosperity for every salesperson who looks the problems of today squarely in the eye and asks these questions and then changes their current methods to adapt to the answers:

1. How do I have to change what I do to be competitive in this new marketplace?
2. How can I become more customer-focused and provide what the customer wants?
3. How can I influence the organisation whose products I sell to do the same and to produce new products and services that are focused on the customer and not the organisation?

Speaking of competition, let me suggest that the concept of 'beating your own best performance' is one very simple and effective way of focusing your time and talents where the payoff will be the highest. Let's start with the concept of beating our own best performance as a way of raising productivity. Remember, whatever you do in life, it is likely you will eventually have to do better. That's the nature of life. It is always the same: no matter how well we do, as we progress we need to do better. That's the nature of the job. So commit yourselves to performing at a higher level because performance is our number one sales and management obligation and we must meet that obligation. Meet it now, today, and always. That's the abiding challenge. It's a challenge that strengthens all who embrace it, and weakens those who fight it. It strengthens and rewards you by setting you the task of beating your best previous performances. Your best previous year's result. Your best previous month. Your best previous week and your best previous day's results. Do it now.

Beating your own best performance is a worthwhile goal because it's for you. It's about you. It's about building a better you. It's not just being done for the business, or the boss, or someone else. It's being done because you and I are by nature self-fulfilling. It's being done because you and I understand that it's forward or backwards — and for us it must always be forward. If you embrace the concept of beating your own best performance then you will have increased the benefits of the past and guaranteed the rewards of the future.

The concept is one thing, the opportunity it creates is another. However, the value, the outcome, the results, depend entirely on you. Because it really is a personal matter of whether you want to accomplish the very highest of standards or whether you're satisfied. If you can respond to this challenge, if you're willing to commit yourselves to this goal then you are almost certain to benefit from the motivation and inspiration it promotes. I can say with certainty that if you embrace the concept of beating your own best performance it's highly unlikely that you will suffer any physical or economic harm. Logic says that if you take part in this competition with yourself you could benefit, whilst if you don't you are almost guaranteed to stay where you are. Performance is the objective but self-achievement is the key to why you should participate. To deny yourselves the opportunity for improvement is to deny existence, for without growth we perish.

So what contribution should you make? If in this current year you want to earn more, own more, be more, see more, or have more, or do more, then go to it and enjoy yourselves. Commit yourselves to these goals. Tell someone about them so that you have someone keeping track of your progress — and then go and make it happen for you. The reality of life seems to be that if you don't care enough or want enough to make your dreams come true, then it is unlikely that anyone else will. Beating your own best performance is a very good way of ensuring your dreams do come true.

Having or not having goals is a major dilemma for many, yet there's really no option. We either have a goal to achieve, or we have a goal not to achieve. Even if we don't take part we have a goal, which seems to be 'I just hope I get lucky'. This type of thinking is brought about because many individuals are fettered by the past rather than being freed by the future. You and I need to be free. Free to dream, free to accomplish, free to do it all our way and one of the best ways is to enter a bargain with life of beating our own best performance.

Let us think of this seminar and this session. The purpose and objective of seminars is to change attitudes, to have each of us go away with an attitude of wanting to be better than our best past performance. One hopes it is a better attitude because we know if there are no changes there are no new results. You came here with the best of intentions. If you leave without making any changes then it was all for nothing. When you're planning, remember, especially today, it's not good enough to only work to part capacity. It's not good enough to sell only enough to get by financially. It's not good enough to simply do enough to survive. The challenge for you and me is to be better than ever before. To commit yourselves to excellence, by demonstrating to every client you deal with that you are willing to go the extra mile to serve them better and in the process achieve your goal of beating your own best performance.

Remember that selling is a creative thinking business and to stay alive in selling you have to keep thinking. You have to present yourselves and your product in a new, better, different and exciting way. It's more important today to do this than ever before. On every front all businesses and managers are being challenged. If your industry is being challenged, you are being challenged — and the major challenge, in my opinion, is for each of us to present ourselves in a more creative, exciting and professional way, because if we don't do this we can't win the day. We need to commit to excellence in everything we do.

I know some have trouble with coming to grips with being a top-class successful individual. They are concerned about all manner of things, the quality of life, fears such as 'I don't want to kill myself with work'. What rot. It's a well-known fact that a mind expands with use. Hard work and mental exercise keep us fit and preserve our youth. I have never met a haggard, worn-out, frustrated millionaire. They all seem amazingly fit and happy to me, but I have observed that society generally is riddled with people who are old before their time, physically and mentally defeated. They never gave their best and they never competed. Commit yourselves to excellence and beat your own best performance. What a fantastic goal. A lifelong pursuit, and if you do it you won't fail.

Tell me, have you ever read a book on how to fail? Have you ever seen a book in a library on how to fail? Can any of you promise me that you can go out tomorrow and buy a book on how to fail? No? Have you ever wondered why? Then I will tell you. You don't have to know how to fail; you simply don't work at succeeding. It is fairly well understood that if you don't become a success, you can easily become a failure, or at least ordinary — and who wants to be ordinary? Be totally goal-oriented. The difference between planning for success and planning for failure is simple: when you plan for success there are positive things that must be done if you want to reach your goal. By not doing anything, by exercising the option of doing nothing you are entering into negative territory. You are abdicating your chance to plan for success. You selected the option of ordinary, average, or failure. If you don't plan to succeed you are certainly planning to be ordinary, by default. Do something. Do anything but default. Don't become a mental cripple. Don't have half a mind to do it.

Make the changes that are necessary and make them today and then do them because in the end each of us must live life one day at a time. You can't do tomorrow what needs to be done today without losing today. You can't do today what should have been done yesterday without sacrificing today. Don't sacrifice today and tomorrow on the altar of procrastination. Plan to live your life one day at a time and to beat your own best performance. What a fantastic idea. The payoff is enormous.

It is a startling and inspiring fact that life will pay any price we ask. But look around: you can see the tragedy of those who trade their days for dimes instead of dollars. Every day as you move around you will see those who ask for so little, their price is so low. Who was it who said — and I believe it to be true — that 'I bargained with life for a penny and life would pay no more'? It could just as easily have been a bargain with life for a million dollars. But if you focus on beating your own best performance life will pay you plenty — as long as you take action now, not tomorrow, *today*.

How easy it is to focus on tomorrow. Tomorrow, we say to ourselves, tomorrow we will get started for sure. Tomorrow we will put that new idea to work, or tomorrow we will change our routine to enable more to be done in the hours available. Tomorrow there will be time. But tomorrow becomes today and we are still on the same old road that leads on and on doing the same things we always do, a slave on the treadmill of our habits.

We attend meetings, seminars and conventions. We hear how others have made a change, how their lives have been enriched by performance, and we plan. We plan to change tomorrow. Tomorrow we will start, always tomorrow. The sadness of our tomorrows that never come. The waste of our promised tomorrows.

Why not start here, today, at this conference while you're listening to this session? Why not start by adopting the concept of thinking big as a way of life? For there is a marvellous magic generated by thinking big. By practising everlasting optimism in the midst of pessimism and worry.

I challenge you to think big. Plan big and act big. Remember always to think big, not about problems but about opportunities. Be receptive to change, to new ideas, especially those changes and ideas that confront you today. Take advantage of them. Then work on them. Step off the treadmill of habit and take charge of your life. To have free choice and not exercise it is to deny your opportunity. Today is your opportunity: don't miss it on the promise of tomorrow. You can have it all now, you don't have to wait for your ship to come in. Ever since you were born it's been waiting at the loading dock of life, full of everything you desire, just waiting for you to unload it. It is filled with all the success that you can imagine — but you have to unload it now. Don't wait for tomorrow, your time is now. Today is your opportunity. Don't miss it on the promise of tomorrow.

Thank you for listening. I hope that in some way I have managed to give you the reasons why you should change now rather than taking what comes. So go to it with every effort you can muster. I wish you all the success that change and innovation can bring.

18. We Never Travel Alone

This is not a presentation that I have made whilst on the speaking circuit. It is a way of thinking that has become part of who I am and how I face life. It is the way I have chosen to build my life, because we do build our own lives by the way we answer life's challenges. Each of us must answer many challenges and solve many difficult problems. If we fail, then we give away the opportunities to shine by overcoming the problems and threats and moving on to success. I hope that in the reading of this book you will have found ways to overcome your difficulties and build upon your successes until they become a way of life for you. I wish you every success that enlightenment can bring.

Life is a journey; like a train trip, it has a beginning, the journey and then the journey's ending, the destination. We humans are always asking, what is life about? What is the purpose of life? Why are we here? The simple answer is that life is about living and living opens the almost limitless possibilities we have of making our journey all we want it to be. We cannot control the start of our journey or its length because the date of our birth and how long we live are not within our control. The best we can do is to adopt a quality of life that will increase our chances of a long, healthy and happy existence.

We can make a train trip alone, but we will never travel alone in our journey through life. It is critical to understand that no matter what we do, what we accomplish, whatever failures or successes come our way, we never travel alone. Even in the greatest of our accomplishments we will, if we are honest, acknowledge that along the way we received willing assistance from others on many occasions. Sometimes we achieved success because of what others did not do. Their inaction made it possible for us to be more effective and achieve great things.

Recently I unexpectedly received an Honorary Doctor of Management degree from a university in Great Britain, which said, 'This award is based on your worldwide contribution to management over the life of your career to date'. An award based on what I had accomplished in a lifetime. Reflecting on my life and why the award came my way, I was conscious of the many people who had helped me in hundreds of ways to accomplish the success that brought the award. I could see quite clearly how at critical times in my life, at some successful and some very threatening moments, many individuals had been there for me, helping as best they could.

I remember when I was only 31 being struck down with a heart attack. It was a very traumatic time for me and my family. I will never forget the help and encouragement I received from many of my friends and associates in what was one of the darkest days of my life. Three people in particular stand out in my memory. The first was my bank manager, who visited and said, 'Don't worry about money; the bank will see you through this problem if you need money.' The second was a lifelong friend who said, 'Don't worry about money; half of what I own is yours if you need it.' The third was a golfing friend who came and said, 'I have 4000 woolies [sheep]. Half of them are yours if you need them.' Fortunately, I never had to take advantage of their kind offers. Those people probably don't realise how much they contributed to whatever success I have had in my chosen field.

During this time we lost our business and had to start again. This new beginning brought a measure of success beyond our wildest dreams. It was as if the power greater than ourselves was saying, 'You need to go through this, because there is a new and more successful life in a different direction that you can now follow.'

We never travel alone and how much help we get from others and from the power greater than ourselves can be measured by how much help we give to others. When helping others to achieve their goals we set up their desire to help us, when possible, to achieve ours. Even in life's toughest times there is always someone willing to give support. Those who have families know only too well how often family have stood by them, even at great cost to themselves. Most of us can remember when we have been the helper and supporter of family or friends who needed care and love. Even in times when we have no one close, when we seem to be all alone and life is tough, there is always the power greater than ourselves that helps us through those times. Those who understand and know how to access their subconscious mind have a reserve of help and understanding that is always there, whenever it is needed. We are never alone if we want help.

Many will recall a time when they were faced with a crisis in their life that seemed to have no ending. Perhaps it threatened a business, or a relationship, perhaps a marriage, even their life, or the life of one of their family. Even in those troubled times somehow they managed to hang on and help came, sometimes from the most unlikely source and in a way that was totally unexpected, as if someone was being directed to help them through a situation that could not be resolved alone.

Faith is a way of thinking that has no limits. Unless we have faith and hope we are isolated. Nowhere to go for help, no one to call on for help. Yet even in the times when hope so easily fades, if we have faith in the power greater than ourselves we can suffer the greatest of problems and still emerge and win our way to success. The power is always with us. Always willing to help if we call. The power does not ask for anything other than belief; and when we give by way of belief, help in ways that we may not have considered will come. It is a case of 'Fear not, I am always with you.'

This spiritual bond with my maker has been with me all my life. Beckoning, calling, as if to say, 'Solving the eternal mystery of life is not the challenge. Just believe and know that I am with you always.'

Every time we give help to someone in need we grow as a person. The very act of helping is in a way a test of our character; it makes us step outside the boundaries of self-considerations. We see the need and we respond, for something deep inside us causes us to remember how help came our way when it was most needed. Now it is time to pay back and give help to someone in need. We never travel alone.

I am sure that during your life there have been times when you have wished that help would come when you had a problem that you could not manage. When life was tough and getting tougher. Trouble or failure is always a possibility in life but it is not the trouble or failure that is the problem. It is the way we respond. Our response can be one of concern that drives us to offer help, or it can be one of indifference that causes us to ignore the prompt to help. If we ignore the opportunity to help we diminish ourselves; if we respond positively we grow.

We never travel alone. Our need to be something better follows us like a shadow, reminding us to be the best we can. Helping others in time of need is life testing us, showing us that there is always the possibility of something better in our life, as if the power greater than ourselves is intent on showing us the way forward. This awareness comes through a lifetime of trust and belief and knowing that we are never alone. The most positive way of dealing with failure when it comes, as surely it will, is to see it as an opportunity to change our tack to something more successful and to make sure we learn from the experience.

Too often we have a picture in our mind of life as a bed of roses, without acknowledging that roses have thorns. Life is like roses. The flowers are beautiful, just like the beauty of life itself. The thorns are the threats and problems of life. We can't have one without the other. We should see life as being wonderful and beautiful, like the flower, and the thorns as being the way life tests us. If we can diminish the hurt of problems by facing them with courage and determination we will be on our way to a more positive and successful life.

Expectations can be a real strength in our life, or they can be trouble from start to finish, depending on whether they are positive or negative. If we cultivate the power of positive expectations as a way of thinking and cut negative expectations from our thoughts we will have tapped into a powerful influence that is capable of transforming our life. As we think, so it will be. Think success and success will come. It is the power of the self-fulfilling prophecy at work in our life. Brian Tracy, business and personal success expert, said that 'Whatever we expect with confidence becomes our own self-fulfilling prophecy.'

In my best-selling book *Yes You Can* there is a complete chapter on how we can build a successful life by using the power of our mind. This is not brainwashing. It is the truth of the power of our mind and how it can be put to work in our life. Why would you reject this power when millions worldwide are using it every day as a way of achieving what they want from life?

The study of the mind, or the lack of it, by the scientific world has held us prisoners as surely as if we were locked behind bars. Bars of ignorance, prejudice and power. The powers of the mind have for too long been the domain of too few. We have been left floundering in ignorance and myth. But now we are breaking free. The possible dream has become a reality for each of us. People in all parts of the world are looking inside themselves with confidence and finding that harnessing the power of the mind is the way to build a successful life for themselves. Personal achievement is what drives them. Why not you if you have not already moved in this direction? Remember, we never travel alone. The power greater than ourselves is always with us, ready to help us on our way to success.

Personal growth must become a way of life for each of us because it is the abiding challenge that the future holds. At some time or other we all fail. We all question what we are focusing on because at some point we are not sure that we are on the right track. Perhaps another way would be better? Life is not always exactly as we want it. The changes come so quickly that as we resolve one problem another problem takes its place. That is just life testing us and at these times our resolve must be strong or we can lose our way. Failure is not all bad if we treat it as an opportunity to learn. If we never learn from our failures we have little hope of eventual success. So it is with our successes; if we don't learn from them we are simply wasting our life.

Could another way have been more successful? If it was a failure was it wrong in principle? Was it too early? Too late? Explore all the possible options. Learning from our successes and failures is the hallmark of how we become successful. Do we know someone whose opinions we respect who could help us with our analysis? There is always someone who is willing to help if we are willing to ask.

There are few of us who at some time or other have not hungered for happiness; who have not experienced a lack of hope for the future, a belief that we are missing out and may never experience true and lasting happiness. When this happens we can easily fall into an even more desperate search for what eludes us, only to discover that the more desperate our search, the more hopeless we feel when we do not find happiness. It takes time to finally understand that perhaps the reason we cannot find and experience happiness is because we are looking in the wrong places. Doing the wrong things. Not paying attention to the issues that could bring permanent happiness into our life. Not being disciplined about the changes we should make that will develop happiness in our life.

It is at these times that we should look for help — and you can be sure help will come, because we never travel alone. At a time when technology is driving us towards separation from our fellow man and into isolation we realise our need for community and our desire and need to be involved with other human beings, to love others as ourselves. One way to find community is to become involved with others who are helping those in need, to show love for our fellow man, to help them through their time of trial, to love your neighbour as yourselves.

The need to be loved is common to all. Do good deeds for others and good deeds will flow to you. If all others forsake us, the power greater than ourselves is always with us, ready to answer our calls for help. Go forth in confidence. Travel in happiness. Give help whenever you can and when you need help it will surely come. Remember, we never travel alone.

Acknowledgements

I'd like to thank the following people for their research, training material, presentations and writing, which have all added to my seminars and to this book:

Michael LeBoeuf, my co-author and friend; Don Mehlig, another friend whose telephone approach I cite in these pages; David McClelland of Harvard University; Joel Barker; Peter Drucker; Douglas Long; Thomas J. Watson; Vince Lombardi, with whom I spent time in the United States; Norman Augustine; Kieren Perkins, whose words come from a television interview; Professor J. Patrick Kelly, K-Mart Chair of Marketing Management at Wayne State University; my friend Denis Waitley; Joe Powell; and Elaine Maxwell.

References

Barker, Joel, *Business of paradigm* (video), Greg Stiever Productions, 2001

Drucker, Peter, *The effective executive*, Harper & Row, New York, 1966

McClelland, D.C., *Power: the inner experience*, New York, Halstead,1975

McClelland, D.C., *The achieving society*, Princeton: Van Nostrand, 1961

McClelland, D.C., Atkinson, J.W., Clark, R.A., & Lowell, E.L., *The achivement motive*, Princeton, Van Nostrand, 1953

Watson, Thomas J.
http://www-03.ibm.com/ibm/history/multimedia/think_trans.html

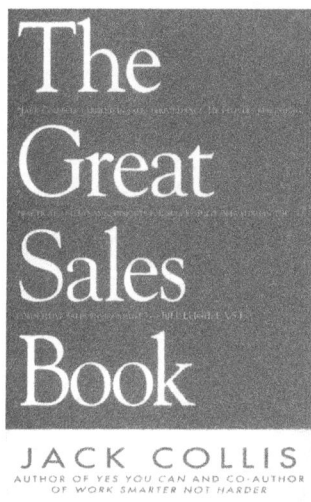

The Great Sales Book

JACK COLLIS

AUTHOR OF YES YOU CAN AND CO-AUTHOR
OF WORK SMARTER NOT HARDER

The Great Sales Book

Not getting the sales figures you need to make budget? Feel as though everyone is slamming the door in your face? Running out of new and innovative ideas for presenting yourself and your product? Don't despair! Jack Collis's book *The Great Sales Book* gives you all the practical help and advice you need to maximise your full selling potential.

Benefit from Jack Collis's years of experience, as he guides you through the psychology of selling, teaches you the art of effective face-to-face communication and gives you excellent tips on how to powerfully present yourself and your product to get the results you want.

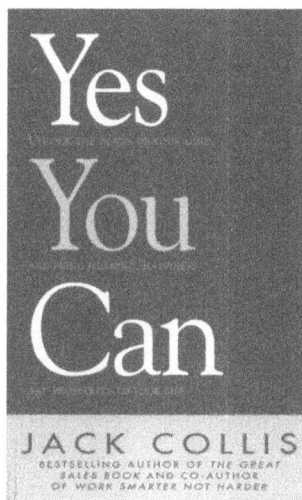

Yes You Can

Jack Collis has more good advice on how to achieve your goals by using the power of your mind. You will learn how to plan and organise yourself effectively to give you the outlook you need to succeed in your chosen field. By focusing directly on what you can do, here and now, every day, *Yes You Can* has more of Jack's wisdom to help you get the most out of your life.

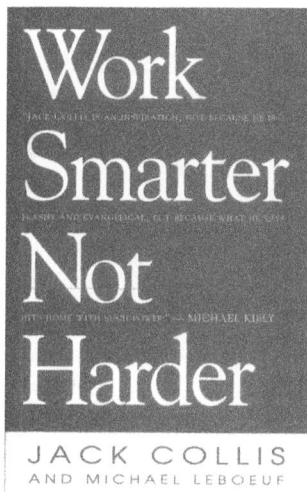

Work Smarter Not Harder

Working too hard? Not getting the fulfilment and rewards you want? With a little guidance from Jack Collis and Michael LeBoeuf, you can find the perfect balance. It's simple. Just work smarter, not harder. *Work Smarter Not Harder* is more than just a business book. It is a clear and effective personal strategy that can help you to get the most out of your life.

www.ingramcontent.com/pod-product-compliance
Lightning Source LLC
Chambersburg PA
CBHW030453210326
41597CB00013B/652